AN INTRODUCTION TO
PAINTING LANDSCAPES

An Introduction to

Painting Landscapes

TECHNIQUE · LIGHT · COLOR · COMPOSITION · STYLE

TED GOULD

CHARTWELL
BOOKS, INC.

A QUINTET BOOK

Published by Chartwell Books
A Division of Book Sales, Inc.
114 Northfield Avenue
Edison, New Jersey 08837

This edition produced for sale in the U.S.A., its
territories and dependencies only.

ISBN 0-7858-0393-9

Reprinted 1999

This book was designed and produced by
Quintet Publishing Limited
6 Blundell Street
London N7 9BH

DEDICATION
For Sue, my wife

Creative Director: Richard Dewing
Designer: Ian Hunt
Project Editor: Stefanie Foster
Editor: Geraldine Christy
Photographer: Paul Forrester

Typeset in Great Britain by
Central Southern Typesetters, Eastbourne
Manufactured by Eray Scan Pte Ltd, Singapore
Printed in Hong Kong, China

CONTENTS

INTRODUCTION

Light, ever changing, is the key to all landscape painting. Objects that make up the natural world are constantly altering their appearance as the light changes. The seasons, too, can bring dramatic differences to a familiar scene, as autumn tints disappear beneath a blanket of snow, or driving rain reduces a spectacular view to a few indistinct shapes. The color of light on objects modifies their intrinsic color. Everyone is familiar with the way light affects the appearance of a mountain range, for instance, at different times of day and in varying weather conditions.

Rapidly changing light caused by unstable weather conditions gives rise to irritation and frustration in painters anxious to "get it down before the light changes." Light can also elicit an emotional response. A bright sunny day with clear blue skies induces a sense of joy, happiness, and peace, whereas a dark, overcast, cold day usually suggests menace, despair, and a sense of isolation.

Artists can evoke these sensations through the use of color that corresponds to light. We can only see the colors in nature through the effects of light – they are inseparable companions.

In this book I will concentrate mainly on the modern conception of landscape in art. Landscape in medieval Europe was largely a

ABOVE *Hunters in the snow* is one of the *Months* series painted by Pieter Bruegel the Elder in 1566. The icy weather can almost be felt in the dull color of the sky.

vehicle for a narrative representing biblical or mythological scenes rather than a representational end in itself. There are similarities here with modern painting, where landscape is used to convey a psychological or painterly response to nature.

The first representational landscapes were painted in the 15th century during the Italian Renaissance. Until then, landscape outside the city walls was generally seen as a hostile environment from which man needed protection. Cultivated walled gardens were used as a kind of theatrical backdrop to figure paintings.

TOPOGRAPHY

As towns and cities grew and the wild forests were tamed and cut down, so the interest in the wider environment grew. It is obvious from paintings done in the Middle Ages that location studies involving intense observation were being made. Dürer (1471–1528) and Altdorfer (c. 1485–1538) were two German artists who produced drawings and paintings where figures were reduced to a minor role in a highly detailed study of nature. Dürer himself is credited with painting the first townscape. In Italy, two Renaissance artists, Giovanni Bellini (c. 1430–1516) and Piero della Francesca (c. 1410–1492), also sought to elevate the importance of landscape to the level of figure painting.

NATURALISM

Dutch 17th-century painting was the first European movement to establish the art of landscape in its own right. Dramatic chiaroscuro effects of light and dark were combined with the depiction of commonplace domestic scenes as Dutch society celebrated the rise of bourgeois living.

Landscape became an accepted subject to paint. The architectural arrangement of shapes in space, the balance of horizontal against vertical, and the overall stillness of paintings by Poussin (1593–1665) embody the principles of the classical tradition in landscape. This line proceeds down through Cézanne and into the abstractionists of the mid-20th century, such as Mondrian.

During the 19th century, the Romantic movement developed. The Romantic artists were concerned with mood, emotion, movement, and effect rather than the purely formal aspects of balance and symmetry in landscape. Nevertheless, the best paintings usually contained elements of all these qualities.

OPPOSITE ABOVE Jacob van Ruisdael showed how to color the northern landscape and the northern sky, with Claudean poetic resonance.

OPPOSITE LEFT *Orpheus and Eurydice* (1650) by Nicholas Poussin uses a landscape formula of dark idealized landscape receding in parallel planes which structure the depth of the painting, while clear vertical and horizontal accents give increased stability to the work. This underlying geometry gives the scene its elegant serenity.

TURNER AND CONSTABLE

These two very different British painters continued the naturalistic tradition, albeit in their own individual ways. Turner (1775–1851) produced grandiose subjects like *The Fighting Temeraire*, while Constable (1776–1837) painted pastoral, almost parochial subjects such as *The Haywain*.

Turner saw the elements of landscape as a unified whole, suffused with an overwhelming light, which merged sky, water, and land as one luminous, swirling form. Constable, infatuated with

ABOVE *Great Falls of Reichenbach* by Joseph Mallord William Turner. This magnificent view of Alpine scenery painted for exhibition in 1804 reveals Turner's use of watercolor for the expression of a vast and solemn romantic theme. The strong tonal contrasts and swirling forms enhance the sense of natural drama.

ABOVE **In works like** *The Haywain* **(1821), Constable struggled against the academic tradition with its Italianate landscapes. He worked extensively directly from nature, before the subject, painting rapidly, with separate strokes and blobs of paint.**

the countryside around Dedham Vale in Suffolk realized the importance of the sky in his work. His use of spectacular tonal contrast, combined with superb brushwork, integrating the sky and land, finally overcame the landscape artists' traditional problem of the "two halves." He loved all the detail of landscape, proclaiming that he had "never seen an ugly thing in his life."

The work of Constable and Turner had a profound influence in France, particularly on Gustave Courbet (1819–77), a realist who painted nature directly as he saw it.

IMPRESSIONISM

Courbet's example led directly to Impressionism. The approach of these artists was not only realistic; their concern was to capture the effect experienced on first seeing a view – in its totality and without undue attention to detail. It was the first movement to be expressly concerned with light. The principal artists were Monet, Renoir, Pissarro, Sisley, Seurat, and Morisot. These painters worked largely outdoors and on location. To seize the precise effects of light and atmosphere on color meant spending long hours enduring the elements. They had to be hardy individuals!

Apart from working directly from the environment, their principal revolutionary development was in the use of color, which they used more purely and brightly than their predecessors. For example, they saw that the shadows in nature are not simply the neutrals black or gray, but blue, violet, and dark green.

Seurat introduced a system known as Pointillism. He called it "ma méthode." Instead of mixing his tones on the palette, he mixed them optically on the canvas. This he did by placing small brush strokes of pure color alongside one another to produce planes of brilliant, vibrating color, when viewed at a distance. For example, he placed dots of primary red alongside pure blue, which then merge in the spectator's eye to appear as violet.

LEFT *Autumn at Argenteuil* (1873) by Claude Monet. This Impressionist painting superbly captures the effect of the sun, low in the sky, on the gold-colored tree foliage at the left of the picture.

BELOW There is a charm and warmth in *Apple Picking* (1888) by Camille Pissarro, which may have been an attempt by him to make his work more popularly acceptable. At the same time, the painting reflects the trend in the 1880s toward the depiction of more solid and larger figures which dominate the scene, and the deployment of more "scientific" theories of color, derived from the example of Seurat.

POST-IMPRESSIONISM

Cézanne (1839–1906) was dissatisfied with the lack of formal considerations in the work of his Impressionist contemporaries. Cézanne's theory that all forms in nature are based on the cone, the sphere, and the cylinder gained him the reputation of being "the father of modern painting." He saw and interpreted the scene in front of him in these terms. He worked on location in the hills around Aix-en-Provence in southern France, using Impressionist color, but he was also influenced by Poussin and the classical tradition in art.

Van Gogh (1853–90) is credited as being the precursor of the entire Expressionist tradition in modern art. To him, the subject was a starting point for his personal response through color to that subject. He has been quoted as saying that he was more concerned with the colors on his palette than those in front of him. Gauguin (1848–93), who started as an impressionist, developed the principles of symbolism. His color and shapes were simplified to produce a more "primitive" effect. He constructed his paintings largely in the studio. Both artists drew their inspiration directly from nature and human experience, rather than from the preconceptions about art held by petit-bourgeois society.

Along with many other artists in the latter part of the 19th century, Van Gogh and Gauguin were influenced by Japanese prints. Flatter, purer color enclosed by a black outline was the manifestation of this influence in European art.

The research into the nature of color by the French scientist Chevreul was to have a major impact on European art. The principle of simultaneous contrast caused artists to substitute the colors they saw before them for colors which make harmonious contrasts. This led directly to the brilliant primary colors used by the Fauvists.

BELOW The Provençal landscape provided the subject matter for hundreds of Cézanne's paintings, and *Mountains in Provence* (*c.*1885) is a perfect summary of the preoccupations and achievements of Cézanne at the beginning of his maturity. Cézanne's concern to give expression to the qualities of the landscape was always balanced by an equal concern for the language of painting. All the features in this composition have a clearly defined role and create an overall harmony in such a way that the removal of any element would destroy the equilibrium.

ABOVE Van Gogh has used long expressive brushstrokes in *Road with Cypress and Star* (1890), transforming the surface of this work – as can be seen in his paintings during his stay in the asylum at St. Rémy – in a way that has been attributed to the series of breakdowns he had suffered.

MODERNISM

From the end of the 19th century, attitudes to landscape painting diverged into a variety of different styles and concepts. Representation for its own sake had been thoroughly explored to the point where sheer observation of nature was no longer enough. The invention of photography was another major factor in the movement away from Naturalism. The photograph was seen as both a threat and a blessing to painters. On one hand, it provided a quick, accurate record of nature and events; on the other, it liberated artists from the burden of pure representation. From this point, painting was never to be the same again.

CUBISM

Braque (1882–1963) and Picasso (1881–1973) took Cézanne's formula of the sphere, cone, and cylinder as a starting point. They, as it were, dissected nature and recomposed it as a series of interlocking planes, the object being to include more than one aspect or angle of a subject in a single picture. The rectangular picture plane was divided into flattish smaller planes involving the elimination of spatial depth.

The Expressionist wing of modernism emerged in France, led by Matisse (1869–1954), and in Germany with Kandinsky (1866–1944) and Franz Marc (1880–1916) as its leaders. Both the French Fauvists and the German

Blue Riders saw nature in terms of pure color. Their painting was characterized by expressive brushwork and violent tonal contrasts. Unlike the Cubists, who never entirely forsook representation, the Germans moved toward abstraction, particularly Kandinsky, who is credited with painting the first entirely abstract picture in 1913. From this point on, new directions for landscape painting began to proliferate. Paul Klee (1879–1940) reduced it to a

BELOW *Smoke Drift* by Timothy Easton. This oil painting beautifully evokes the effects of sunset in autumn. The scene is essentially backlit, putting the objects into silhouette against a bright sky. The leaves on the spruce trees are scumbled with touches of rich color over the background.

ABOVE Hazel Soan's watercolor *Kudo at Goas* creates the arid effects of a watering hole in the African bush. The wet-in-wet technique used for the sky and background contrasts with the dry brushed trees and animals.

series of textural diagrams. Futurism and Surrealism arrived and treated landscape as a symbol for psychological expression. Concepts about the content from within replaced the observable world without. The introduction and juxtaposition of incongruous images within landscape created a shock reaction with the public. The appearance of the Surrealist movement in Europe was a major force throughout the 1920s and 30s, involving a large number of artists: André Breton (1896–1966) and followers in France, René Magritte (1898–1967) in Belgium, and the flamboyant Spaniard Salvadore Dali (1904–89) just about everywhere. Breton is credited as being the founder of the Surrealist movement. Paradoxically, he was a

poet, not a painter!

The new industrial power becoming visible in the environment inspired Marinetti (1876–1944) and the Futurists in Italy to produce images of dynamism.

The migration of the Surrealists to the U.S.A. at the outbreak of World War II caused a revolution in American art, culminating in the appearance of Abstract Expressionism. Landscape was used as a vehicle to express notions about color and brushwork, harking back in some cases to its use in medieval Europe.

The fascination with the constantly changing visible world has maintained its hold on painters everywhere, although the discoveries of the last hundred

years have influenced style and approach. Photography, originally seen as the usurper of representational art, is now widely used as a valuable means of obtaining source material for painters. The Photo-realists actually copy photographs at very large size in minute detail. The photograph is now almost as indispensable to the traveling artist as the traditional sketchbook. Leonardo da Vinci said that "drawing is the root of all science." It is also the prerequisite of all good painting, so do lots of it!

1

MATERIALS AND EQUIPMENT

The choice of materials and equipment available to the artist is vast, and here I will concentrate only on the essential items that will allow you to attempt similar landscape projects to those demonstrated later. I am also concerned that artists should not be overwhelmed by the sheer variety and complexity of all the possible technical aids to painting.

Technical virtuosity is not an end in itself. The most successful paintings have often been made with limited materials and equipment – five colors, three or four brushes, a simple piece of board or paper – and plenty of inspiration!

Expense is another good reason for restricting the selection you start out with. Art materials are not cheap. Care and proper use of materials and equipment are very important. If they are looked after, they will go further and last longer.

SKETCHBOOKS

An essential item of equipment for any painter is the sketchbook. It should be like a good companion – always there when needed, providing a reservoir of information and ideas. The type I prefer is spiral bound and contains sheets of cartridge paper (acid-free) for quick sketches, size 5 × 8 inches. This can be carried with you and used for getting down details, notes on color, and ideas for future paintings. There is also a large choice of watercolor sketchbooks; these are ideal for working on

location or in the studio and are available in a variety of sizes from 5 × 8 inches to 16 × 24 inches. A good-quality watercolor book containing sheets of heavyweight acid-free paper can be used for the final paintings.

ABOVE *Allotments* **by Mike Bernard. This pencil drawing demonstrates the range of tone and texture that can be achieved solely with the use of a 3b pencil.**

BELOW *Reservoir in the Wye Valley.* **Watercolour by the author. Done on location, this sketchbook study utilises both the wet-in-wet and wet-in-dry techniques to create the effects of light.**

OILS

Paints

I suggest a selection of colors that will serve you for a variety of subjects in different light and weather conditions: Permanent Violet, Alizarin Crimson, Cadmium Red Light, Cadmium Yellow Medium, Naples Yellow, Burnt Sienna, Permanent Green, Chrome Oxide Green, Cerulean Blue, Ultramarine Blue, Cobalt Blue, Yellow Ocher, Burnt Umber, Sap Green, Cadmium Orange, Payne's Grey, Lamp Black, Titanium White.

Palettes

In addition to wood, there are also plastic (plexiglass) palettes, masonite board coated with acrylic primer, and tear-off paper palettes. These are useful for location work. I use a large wooden palette for studio work and a lightweight masonite board when working outside.

Brushes

Brushes are all based on three shapes: round, flat, and filbert, with a special fan shape for texturing and blending tones. They are all produced in hog's hair bristle, sable, or synthetic bristle. The best quality are hog's hair and sable, but the synthetics have improved in quality over recent years and they are quite satisfactory. The price is usually a good indicator of quality and durability. Most brush brands are made in both "long hair" and "short hair" versions. Long-hair hog bristles are the best for applying large areas of color and for accentuated brush marks. Use the sables for smoother effects and putting in fine detail.

ABOVE **Glazes of color are the basis of this picture, *The Church at Wareham*, by the author.**

ABOVE ***Distant Bonfire in the Iris Field.* Oil by Timothy Easton.**

Palette knives

Palette knives are made in a variety of shapes and sizes. They serve two main purposes: mixing the paint on the palette and applying paint to the canvas. The broad or flat design is for mixing and the pointed, angled type is for knife painting. A useful item for your studio is a mahlstick. This is a length of wood dowel with a soft pad at one end. Its function is as a hand rest when painting straight lines or fine details.

Solvents and Binders

The most commonly used and readily obtainable solvents and binders for oil painting are linseed oil, poppy oil, and refined spirit of turpentine. They can be used separately or mixed together for thinning paint. Mixing pure linseed oil with your paints produces a glossy, lustrous effect, but it is slow drying. Turpentine on its own leaves

ABOVE Solvents for oils: refined linseed oil, distilled turpentine, mineral spirits, and poppy oil.

the painting matte and flat in appearance, although it will dry faster. The "household" type of untreated turpentine or mineral spirits is not suitable for paint mixing and should be used only for cleaning brushes.

Supports

Any material that can be primed and prepared may be used for oil painting: fabric, wood, cardboard, masonite, or paper. The primer commonly used is white acrylic. There are a variety of ready-made supports available, including stretched canvas, canvas boards, and canvas paper. Canvas boards and canvas pads are handy for location work where portability is important. The traditional oil-painting support is primed cotton canvas stretched over a wood frame.

Easels

An easel is essential for any painter working directly from observation. Having the support vertical enables the artist to make instant comparisons with the subject and the painted image. There are a number of different types and sizes of easels. Small portable metal easels are lightweight, but tend to be unstable in windy conditions. Wooden fold-up easels with telescopic legs are ideal for location work. The ultimate for portability is probably the combination sketch-box easel. When unfolded and set up, this device consists of a paintbox with drawer and a small vertical easel with adjustable legs. For studio work involving larger paintings, there are the radial easel and the studio easel.

ABOVE *The Park in Autumn.* Oil by the author. An example of the alla prima technique.

A SELECTION OF MATERIALS FOR OIL PAINTING

1 A starter set of oil colors
2 Selection of artist's oil colors
3 Selection of brushes, bristle, and sable hair – round, flat, and filbert shaped
4 Stretched canvas
5 Canvas boards
6 Wood palettes
7 Crank-handled palette knives

ACRYLICS

Acrylic paints were first developed by Mexican mural painters in the 1930s. These artists were seeking a durable paint that would withstand harsh weather conditions. Acrylics consist of pigment bound in a synthetic resin. They are quick drying, and when dry they are lightfast and produce a hard matte surface. In warm temperatures an acrylic painting will dry within minutes, so that it can be taken off the easel and packed away in the time it takes to wash the brushes. This fast-drying characteristic makes acrylics a good choice for location work. There is a retarder available to slow down drying, which is essential if you wish to blend colors on the canvas. Acrylics have most of the characteristics of oil paint. Their quality is comparable, and they offer a similar range of colors. Acrylics may be used for underpainting, impasto, and palette-knife work. However, due to the drying speed, you have to work quickly, because you cannot easily scrape the paint off and start again. Used straight from the tube, acrylics behave in a similar way to thick gouache paints. Heavily diluted with water, they can be brushed on in broad washes, achieving virtually the same effect as with watercolor. Generally, acrylics are cheaper than oil, making them attractive to students and those on a limited budget.

Paint

It is advisable for all painters to use a consistent selection of colors in all media; therefore, I would suggest the same selection as listed in the oil section on page 18.

ABOVE *The Garden in Spring.* **Acrylic by the author. Planes of color overlaid with sparks of brilliant color create the seasonal feel.**

Palettes

There are two kinds of palettes suitable for acrylics: plastic and the "wet" palette. Wood is not recommended, because it is more difficult to clean when the paint has dried. The "wet" palette is an ingenious device designed to keep the paint workable for longer periods. It is basically a plastic box with a layer of blotting paper placed on the inside. This is then soaked with water and a second sheet is placed on top, so retaining a damp surface on which to lay out the colors. If the lid is replaced when finishing for the day, the colors can remain workable until the following morning.

Mediums

Various mediums are available for acrylics. They are: gloss, matte,

ABOVE Gerry Baptist's contrasting, brilliant primary colors give a luminosity and overall glow to this acrylic painting *Provençal Landscape*. The use of diagonals and triangular shapes in the buildings produces a dynamic composition.

retarder, and gel. They are mixed in specified proportions with the paint according to your preference.

Supports

As with oil, almost any surface can be used for acrylic painting: canvas, wood, metal, masonite, cardboard, and paper. It is not essential that a primer is used, except on porous surfaces such as canvas and cardboard. The universal primer is acrylic primer.

Brushes

The same selection of brushes may be used for acrylics as for oil painting. Keep your brushes in a jar of water while working and wash them out thoroughly afterward. Paint-hardened brushes can be softened by soaking in denatured alcohol for about 12 hours.

2

WINSOR GOLD – Long Flat – Pure Hog   10

2

5

2

2

ARTISTS'
ACRYLIC
COLOUR
WINSOR & NEWTON
Azo Yellow Medium
(Arylid - Yellow G)
Jaune Moyen Azo
Echtgelb, mittel
Amarillo Mediano (Azo)
Giallo medio (azoico)
Permanence A SL S2
60 ml ℮ 2 US fl oz

1

4

Naphthol Crimson
WINSOR & NEWTON
ARTISTS'
ACRYLIC
COLOUR
Rouge Naphthol
Carmin
Rouge Naphthol Carminé
Karmesin
Carmesí natlolp
Permanence A SL S2
60 ml ℮ 2 US fl oz

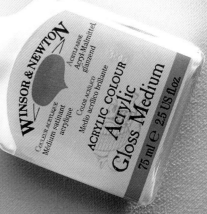

A SELECTION OF MATERIALS FOR ACRYLIC PAINTING
1 Tubes of artist's acrylic paint
2 Selection of brushes, bristle, and sable hair – flat and fan shapes
3 Bottles of matte and gloss medium
4 Small plastic palette
5 "Stay wet" palette
6 Water jar
7 Palette knife
8 Palette knife

WATERCOLOR AND GOUACHE

Paints

The quality of watercolors varies considerably, so it is advisable to buy from reputable manufacturers. Check that the term "Artists'" appears somewhere on the label; then you can be assured of good quality. Watercolor is pigment, finely ground and suspended in water with gum arabic as the binder. As a general rule, it is not necessary to have as many colors on the palette as with oils or acrylics, because of the "wash" characteristic of watercolors. Working wet-in-wet produces tints and shades by the very nature of the medium. Some distinguished watercolorists of the past have not used more than six or seven colors. Again, select your colors from those that you use for other painting media or from the list for oils on page 18.

Watercolors are available in small cakes (called half pans), tubes, and bottles. Both tubes and half pans can be bought separately or in tin boxes, which also serve as palettes. They are all fast drying and do not change their color value when dry. Gouache paint can be described as opaque watercolor. It has this opacity because of the addition of an inert white pigment, which gives it a handling quality similar to matte acrylics. As with acrylics, it is fast drying, but unlike acrylics it can be soaked off for changes or corrections. Watercolor obtains its pure brilliance through transparency, whereas with gouache the flat, bright color is reflected back from the surface of the paint itself. Both watercolor and gouache are suitable for making quick, on-the-spot studies. Watercolor is preferable when the object is to capture the transient qualities of light and mood. I prefer gouache for

small-scale color compositions that are to be scaled-up later into larger paintings in oil or acrylics. Water-soluble crayons are also a useful medium for quick studies. They produce an effect similar to watercolor, but involve less equipment. All you need is a small container for water and a brush to move the color around after you have made a sketch.

Palettes

Most watercolorists carry with them a box, which also functions as a palette when opened out. These are available in various sizes, some large enough to contain one or two brushes. For studio use, larger ceramic or plastic palettes are also available, but a large dinner plate is as good as anything.

ABOVE *Fish River Canyon.* Hazel Soan's watercolor combines sensitive drawing with delicate color washes.

Brushes

Brushes are made in a variety of types from broad flat squirrel and goat hair to very fine pointed sable brushes. The type of brush you use will directly influence your style and the final effects obtained. The finest quality brushes are the sables. These are made from mink fur and are expensive, but they are the most durable and long-lasting. A good, fine-pointed sable brush is ideal for washes and fine detail. Flat, chisel-shaped sables are also produced specially for paintings requiring large areas of wash color. Because of the adaptability of the pointed sable, it is not generally necessary to buy very small sizes; sizes 2 to 12 will do most tasks. If funds are low, you can try out some of the synthetic brushes, but beware that you do not end up with the poorest quality, because they will not be capable of achieving the subtle effects you may want.

Water

For the perfectionist, distilled water is safer than tap water. Tap water can be too hard or too soft, and it can affect the paper and paints. Always have at least two containers: one for mixing paint, the other for cleaning your brushes.

Papers and boards

A lot of work can be done directly in watercolor sketchbooks – especially when working on location. These are available in a variety of papers, as described on page 17. The choice of both papers and papers mounted on board is extensive. They are obtainable under the following headings referring to their manufacturing technique: Hot Pressed, Cold

ABOVE **Mist in the Mountains. Watercolor by Kenneth Swain.**

Pressed or NOT, and Rough. Hot Pressed has a smooth surface and is suitable for line and wash paintings, but the absence of grain makes it less attractive to watercolor painters, who prefer the "tooth" of the other two. Hand-made papers are expensive, but they are of high quality. They are normally made of pure linen rag. There are also a number of more "exotic" papers found in specialist stores. Among them is Japanese rice paper, which is absorbent and has to be handled delicately.

The weight and thickness of watercolor paper is an important consideration. Paper weights for

watercolor range from 90 pounds to 300 pounds. The heavier weights (150 pounds and above) may be worked on directly, but the lighter or thinner papers must be stretched to avoid buckling when washes are applied to the surface. The best weight and surface for general use would be a 100-pound cold-pressed surface cartridge paper. To avoid the need for stretching, some papers are produced in board form. The paper is mounted on a cardboard support, which guarantees that the surface will remain flat from the start of a painting to the finish.

**A SELECTION OF
WATERCOLOR AND GOUACHE
MATERIALS**

1 Tubes of artists' watercolor
  paint
2 A boxed set of watercolor
  tubes
3 Tubes of designers'
  gouache color
4 A watercolor box
  (containing half-pans,
  palette, water bottle, a
  brush, and a sponge)
5 A selection of sable
  brushes
6 One wash brush
7 A ceramic palette
8 A ring-bound watercolor
  sketchbook
9 A sheet of watercolor board
10 A piece of wax

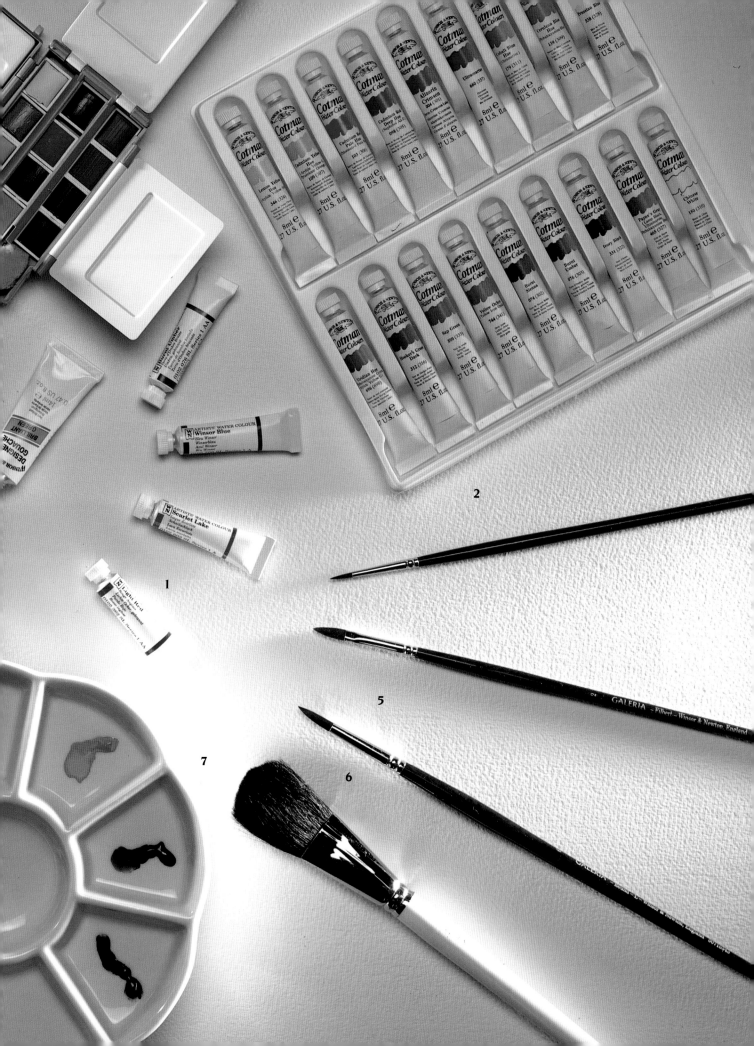

PASTELS

Colors

A very wide range of colors, numbering hundreds, are manufactured as pastels. They are produced as square or round sticks of pigment and as pencils. A large number of colors are made because pastels cannot be mixed on a palette. Thus the artist needs a wider selection of tints than is the case with watercolor or oils.

Pastels can be purchased either singly, or boxed in sets. A reasonable choice for those just starting to use pastels would be a boxed set of 48 tints. Pastels are manufactured in three grades: soft, medium, and hard. The soft grade, as its name suggests, is best suited for laying large areas of color and overlaying, while the hard versions are intended for linear drawing. Oil pastels are an alternative to the traditional type. They are growing in popularity because they are stronger and less likely to break during use. The oil pastel produces an effect akin to oil painting, which makes it ideal for preliminary sketches on location.

Sketching with pastels

Pastels are lightweight and easily portable. They are fast to work with and, of course, there is no drying time involved. These qualities make them an ideal medium for color sketching without the paraphernalia of oil or watercolor painting.

Supports

Watercolor paper or rough cartridge paper, Ingres paper, and various cover papers are used as a support for pastels. In fact, any paper or board that has a textured, fibrous surface that will accept the pastel grains can be used. Papers tinted with a neutral color are also popular with pastel artists, who often prefer to work on a base color rather than pure white.

Equipment

A drawing board or an easel may be used. It is advisable not to work flat, as the pastel dust tends to accumulate and obscure the picture as it progresses. When using a drawing board, set it at an angle, so that the dust will fall downward, away from the picture.

Other items you may need when working are: a tightly rolled piece of paper to use as a pastel spreader, a soft duster, a kneaded putty eraser, a sharp knife, and a fixative spray.

ABOVE **Pastel by Nancy Green. This picture demonstrates the richness and subtlety of pastel skilfully used.**

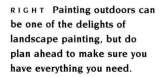

RIGHT **Painting outdoors can be one of the delights of landscape painting, but do plan ahead to make sure you have everything you need.**

BASIC TECHNIQUES

Technique is not a thing which can be taught – it has to be discovered. Every artist has to find the method of painting a picture which suits him or her best. This takes time and a willingness to experiment with and understand the medium which is being used.

Your technique becomes your style, and your personal style is the quality that distinguishes your own work from that of others. Study the technique of good artists and note the methods they use to obtain their effects. There are a wealth of explanatory art books and magazines which can serve as a guide.

The ability to develop a repertoire of techniques is essential as an aid to expression in the creative process. It is important also to gain a knowledge of the possibilities as well as the limitations inherent in the different media. When all these factors are understood, the artist can then be fully in control of the means of expression, rather than being controlled by them!

What follows is a description of the basic techniques, which are, as it were, the classic methods that have evolved throughout the long history of painting. The demonstrations later on in this book illustrate a number of other techniques which have been adopted by contemporary artists working in the various media.

USING OILS AND ACRYLICS

There are two basic methods of painting a picture in oils or acrylics: alla prima and glazing.

Alla prima

This is the most direct method. The painting is usually completed from start to finish in one session. It is particularly widely used for landscape, where working on location under changing light and weather conditions is always a hazard. The exact method adopted by different artists varies a little, but I will explain the generally accepted procedure.

No preliminary studies are done other than a lightly sketched drawing in charcoal or thinned paint applied directly to the painting support. The support is usually white with no base color. The paint is applied right across the picture, either in small brush strokes or in broad areas of colors, followed by blending and joining tones, with a few touches to finish the work. As the painter is working quickly with this method the viscosity (liquidness) of the paint is important. It has to be rather like thick cream – supple, yet at its full brilliance. To achieve this, the paint should be diluted with a little oil and turpentine on the palette *before* starting the painting. This technique was the one favored by the *en plein air* Impressionists.

BELOW **Picnic in the Park by the author. Painted in oil alla prima, the band of shadow under the trees, broken with dappled light, contrasts with the sunlit background.**

Glazing

Glazing involves working with successive transparent layers of diluted paint, so that each layer allows the color beneath to remain visible. For those who prefer to build up their picture by stages, glazing is the classic method. With a few exceptions, all painters since Van Gogh have worked in this way. As this technique takes longer to execute, it is normally used for painting in the studio.

It may involve scaling up a sketch or study for transfer to the full-size painting support. The drawing is then made using charcoal or diluted paint. This is followed by a thinned layer of paint indicating areas of light and dark. When this is dry, the entire painting is covered by successive layers of paint, except for the very lightest areas. It is important to allow each layer to dry sufficiently before adding the next; this prevents the underpainting from being disturbed and "muddied." Finally, highlights and definition lines are applied using thicker, impasto paint. Usually white is absent from the glazes to retain their transparency.

Glazing is suitable for oil, acrylic, and watercolor painting.

BELOW *Girl by the Edge of a Wood.* **The author used successive glazes of thinned oil color to achieve richness and tonal depth. Finally, bright patches of thick color create the effect of dappled light.**

Impasto

Impasto is normally the final stage in a painting. Paint is mixed thickly, sometimes straight from the tube. This technique is frequently used as an overpainting to enrich the color and give texture to a picture produced by glazing. It is suitable for oil and acrylic painting.

RIGHT A vigorous impasto painting by the author. *Summer Garden* began with a base drawing in thin color onto which thicker paint was applied. The layers were gradually built up before employing the palette knife for the final touches.

BELOW *Autumn in Hadley* is another impasto oil by the author. This time the method first used was alla prima, beginning with all the violet and blue areas behind the foliage. A variety of browns and yellows were mixed in thicker paint for the foreground foliage.

Palette knife

A version of impasto painting, but applied with a knife, this technique is generally used as an overpainting to increase surface texture. Large amounts of paint are first mixed on the palette, then applied to the support using an angled, pointed palette knife. Sand or sawdust is sometimes mixed into the paint to increase its bulk and texture. The result usually has the appearance of a spontaneous, expressionistic style. Suitable for oil and acrylic.

RIGHT *St. Paul's from Ludgate Hill.* Oil by Kenneth Swain. This splendid picture has been produced almost exclusively with the palette knife. The red London buses serve both as a focal point and a lead-in to the dome of St. Paul's Cathedral in the background.

RIGHT *Chania Harbour* by the author seemed to demand the use of the palette knife to achieve the scintillating reflections of brightly lit buildings seen in the water of this Cretan port.

Scumbling

Frequently used by the Impressionists, scumbling is the best method for putting the finishing touches to a painting. It is suitable for subjects requiring bright highlights appearing on water. The method is to drag, or roll, a brush heavily loaded with dryish paint across the required parts of the picture, leaving the underpainting visible. Suitable for oil and acrylic.

ABOVE *The Poplars, the Four Trees* (1891) by Claude Monet. Monet built up his painting in layers, usually allowing parts of the previous layer to show through by separating his brush strokes. The final layer utilizes thick, purer color flicked and dragged onto the surface.

RIGHT *Autumn Trees* by the author. The nature of this subject is ideal for the scumbling technique. The tree trunk and the tree shape were first drawn in thinned oil color and when it was dry, thick paint was dragged or dabbed across the foliage to produce the pure autumn tints.

Scratching

This is simply scraping off paint to reveal the underpainting and leave a textured effect. The point of a palette knife or the tip of a brush handle was frequently used by the Cubists to draw into wet paint. This is difficult with acrylics where drying time is so short. Most suitable for oil.

RIGHT **This detail of** *Autumn at Argenteuil* **by Claude Monet shows his use of scratching at the completion of the painting. The paint layers have been scored back to the canvas surface, probably because he felt that the tones were too dense and he wanted to stress the effect of movement and reflected light.**

BELOW **Extensive use of scratching with the tip of a palette knife is evident in Kenneth Swain's dramatic oil** *Welsh Chapel***. The technique has been used to stress the shape of the angular forms and to create texture.**

USING WATERCOLORS

Watercolor is probably the oldest painting medium in the history of art. It dates back over thousands of years to the ancient Egyptian civilization. If you are prepared to persevere with the technique and the handling of the material, watercolor can also be one of the most satisfying. The pigment is finely ground and suspended in a binder of gum arabic. It is transparent, contains no white, and, in the hands of a skilled artist, can produce the most subtle and delightful effects. This very transparency, however, means that every mark will show through successive washes of paint – a characteristic that led a painting teacher of mine to remark that "when you put down a line, you're stuck with it."

There are several other forms of water-based media, including distemper, fresco, and gouache.

The two principal techniques involved are wet-in-wet and glazing.

Wet-in-wet
Paint is applied in diluted washes to damp or dry paper. Additional washes of varying color are then worked into the first wash before it is dry. The extremely fluid nature of this method makes it difficult to predict exactly the outcome, but it can result in a "happy accident."

ABOVE *The Fisherman* by Kenneth Swain. Watercolor washes of delicate color have been applied to a dampened surface. The figure and its reflection were put in at the end when the background was dry.

BELOW The paper was first dampened in this garden study by the author. Washes of color were dropped onto the surface before applying stronger tints for the blossoms and foliage.

Glazing

This is the classic watercolor technique, which is more precise than "wet-in-wet." A light sketch drawing is made onto white paper. Successive washes are applied, starting with the palest overall color, leaving the bright highlights white. The washes progressively darken and enrich the surface until the final wash is applied only on the areas of deep shadow.

RIGHT This example of glazing with watercolor by the author demonstrates the richness of color and depth of tone that can be achieved. The study also includes some wet-in-wet technique in the foreground. Some initial planning is necessary when using the glazing technique.

Line and wash

This is a good technique for sketching on location, because you can make a study quickly. Only a minimum of color is needed, with line added to define forms.

There are two methods of approach:
1 Make a preliminary line drawing on the support, then apply washes of color up to the boundary lines, still retaining the line beneath.
2 Apply color washes first, then when it is dry, draw the lines on top to accentuate the forms and indicate shadow areas. Pencil, ink, conté pencil or charcoal may be applied for the line work.

RIGHT A camping vacation provided the opportunity for the author to produce a quick line and wash sketch. In this study, pale washes were first applied to a damp ground and, when dry, the line was added to define the forms and strengthen tone.

Blotting and sponging

Sponges are indispensable for most watercolor techniques, to remove excess paint and lighten tones (natural sponges are preferable). Dipped in paint, they can be used to add color to washes and create textures. Blotting paper will soak off washes almost down to the surface.

1 The soft, irregular texture of a sponge makes it a highly versatile tool particularly suited to rendering the texture of tree foliage. In this first stage of the painting, the artist begins by loosely washing in the shapes of the trees with pale tones of sap green.

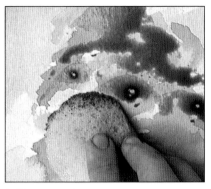

2 The artist mixes up a more intense wash of sap green and Payne's grey for the mid-tones of the foliage. A rounded sponge is dipped in clear water, squeezed out until it is just damp, and pressed into the pool of color on the palette and then used to deposit a mottled pattern of dark tones over the dried underlayer.

3 The painting is allowed to dry, after which slightly darker tones of Payne's grey and sap greens are sponged onto the tree shapes and a few slender branches indicated with a rigger brush.

Masking fluid

Masking fluid is employed extensively by some artists. Its purpose is to mask out those areas that are to remain white, or to retain the purity of an underlying color wash. Masking fluid can be painted on, stippled with a toothbrush, or spattered. It dries quickly and can then be painted over. When the painting is dry, it can easily be removed by gently rubbing it with a finger.

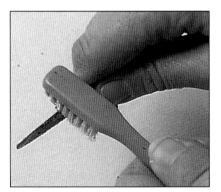

1 A small quantity of masking fluid is lifted from the tinting saucer with an old toothbrush. The loaded brush is dragged against the edge of a palette knife so that flecks of masking fluid are spattered onto the surface of the paper and allowed to dry before overpainting.

2 After dampening the paper, the artist mixes a wash of raw and burnt sienna and uses a broad brush to create an irregular shape on the paper.

3 The paint is broken by the now-dry droplets of masking fluid.

STRETCHING PAPER

Light- or medium-weight papers tend to buckle when wet paint is applied, but they won't do this if they are stretched. Stretching paper may seem a chore, but there are two excellent reasons for doing it. One is that you can save a good deal of money, because light papers are considerably less expensive than heavy ones, and the other is that stretched paper is more pleasant to work on – it is frustrating to paint over ridges caused by buckling. Stretching isn't difficult, but you need to do it well in advance of painting. The paper has to be soaked and will take at least two hours to dry thoroughly.

1 Draw light pencil lines about half an inch from the edges of the paper to help you put the tape on straight.

2 Immerse the paper briefly in water, turning it over once to make sure both sides are evenly damp. You can do this in a bathtub, sink, or plastic tray.

3 Place the paper on the board and smooth it with a damp sponge to remove any creases or air bubbles.

4 Cut four pieces of tape roughly to length and dampen each one just before use by running it over the sponge. Don't make it too wet or it may stretch and tear.

5 Place the strip around all four edges, smoothing it with your hand as you go. Trim the corners with the scissors or a sharp knife, and stand the board upright until the paper is completely dry.

USING GOUACHE

Gouache could be described as the commercial artist's watercolor. It is an extremely flexible medium, which may be used in heavily diluted form like watercolor, or as opaque body color resembling acrylic or matte oil painting. Thus, all the techniques previously described for watercolor can also be used for gouache painting.

Dry brush

An old brush with splayed bristles or a fan-shaped brush may be used for this technique. Normally, the brush is first dabbed on a piece of cloth after dipping it in the paint to prevent overloading and losing the required effect. Dry brush is particularly good for adding textures to grasses, winter trees, etc.

Flat color

Because of its opacity, gouache is ideal for laying flat areas of color. The brush should be well loaded with paint with about the viscosity of light cream. The color is then laid down in horizontal strokes, keeping the edge wet to receive the next stroke. If the edge dries before this, the result will be "streaky." However, with gouache it is

possible to soak off mistakes and overpaint again.

Gouache lift

This technique produces an effect akin to a lino or wood cut. The principle is based on an underpainting of thick gouache (water-based) and a complete overpainting of India ink (insoluble). Line and wash board is the best surface to work on. When

ABOVE Two gouache studies by the author show the use of flat color broken with some finer lines to create texture. The red gate acts as a focal point.

complete and absolutely dry, the painting is placed under running water and gently "washed off." The gouache dissolves and "lifts" the ink from the surface – except in those areas *not* first painted with gouache. A black negative effect is left on the board.

ABOVE *Trees* by the author demonstrates extensive use of dry-brushed color. Thick dryish gouache color has been dabbed onto pale background tints, creating a sense of transparency.

USING PASTELS

It is important to remember that pastels, unlike oil or watercolor, cannot be mixed on the palette. Different tints of color can only be obtained by using another pastel or, to a limited degree, smudging or blending on the support.

Because pastels cannot be mixed before using, it is essential before starting to select all the colors you will need to complete a painting. They should be laid out according to color and tone. A piece of corrugated cardboard is ideal for this purpose.

The strokes made by a pastel vary enormously, depending on the angle at which they are held and the manner in which they are used. Held lengthwise and flat against the support, they produce a wide band of color. Held upright, they can be used for medium-width strokes of color and for "stubbing in" more brilliant dots of color. If broken in half, very fine lines can be drawn with the edge onto the support. Pressing down on the pastel will result in larger amounts of color filling the paper grain and giving a more "solid" look to the mark. Conversely, light pressure results in a smaller deposit of pastel, with more texture and background showing through.

Pieces of pastel can be ground down to make a powder. This can be done with a piece of wood or a metal spoon and then applied to the support with a soft tissue or brush; the technique is useful for obtaining background tints.

Most artists adopt either of two methods of painting:
1 Layering. Broad strokes of pastel are laid one over the other, building up to a rich, dense finish. It is usually necessary to fix each layer before the next is applied, although this can be avoided with soft pastels.
2 Linear. Strokes of pastel are placed all around the picture with little or no attempt to blend. Additional strokes are then applied using different colors until the entire picture is densely covered with long and short strokes. This method is usually adopted for work on a tinted background support, where the intention is to retain the neutral color in the final painting.

Protecting a pastel painting

Pastel is the most vulnerable of the painting media. A picture is easily spoiled if the surface is accidentally touched or if it is placed uncovered in a portfolio. Spray lightly with a fast-drying fixative, before covering the work with a sheet of tissue paper.

The paper should be anchored to the support, or wrapped around it to prevent rubbing during transportation.
Note Be sparing with the fixative, because too much can cause some colors to darken, and some, notably white, may disappear altogether.

BELOW **Nancy Green's delightful pastel painting is reminiscent of Monet, with tints of pink and blue in the background contrasting with green and yellow in the foreground.**

3
SKETCHING

Sketches are the principal reference source for the landscape painter. The sketchbook is the artist's personal visual dictionary, containing everything that might be used in later works, from thumbnail studies of leaves and grasses to compositional drawings in preparation for large-scale paintings.

Sketching is also a pleasure in itself. Every painter has experienced the urge to make a quick visual statement, when suddenly confronted by a superb view or an intriguing object, a scene that demands to be drawn on the spot and with whatever materials are on hand.

Quite apart from compiling your own visual handbook, sketching is vital to the artist's personal creative development. It is like a private sanctuary where experiments can be made and ideas explored, free from public scrutiny. The dedicated artist always carries a sketchbook or notebook with him wherever he goes. A small ring-bound sketchbook is ideal for the purpose as it slips easily into a coat pocket or a small bag.

A phenomenon associated with sketching is that the sketch often appears more natural and satisfying than the finished painting made from it. This is because we are stimulated by the first sight of the scene and make the drawing without preconception. We are also in an unconcerned, relaxed state of mind, enabling us to work quickly, without self-conscious thought about quality or "getting it right."

Of course, you can work in any medium to produce a sketch. The quick drawing that we have been discussing is probably best done with a pencil or pen, but color can be used as well. When I decide to make a day of it, I take a small box of watercolors or some water-soluble pencils, even on occasion oils or acrylics and a portable easel. The difference between setting up to do a full-scale painting and a sketch is that I will move my

position several times during the day. That is why I need the most portable of equipment. Many "plein air" artists, including some of the Impressionists, have the practice of sketching in the whole picture loosely in thinned color. They finish the painting with thicker, more brilliant color in their studio with the support of sketches and studies.

ABOVE *Trees and a stretch of water on the Stour* (1836–7) by John Constable. Here we can see the influence Constable's treatment of light had on the French painters.

Water-soluble pencils and felt-tip pens are very handy tools for doing quick color and tonal sketches. You need a small covered water container and a brush to dissolve the color and spread the tone.

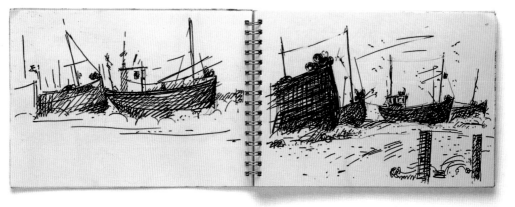

ABOVE **Another quick pen sketch by the author sitting on the quayside. A fountain pen was used for the line drawing and then the ink was smeared and spread with a piece of damp cloth to create tone and to soften the line.**

ABOVE *Houses by a Canal* **by the author. This study is another example of the line and wash technique. The line drawing was made first using a 2b pencil. Only the basic shapes of the houses and canal bank were indicated lightly. Watercolor was then washed in over the line.**

LEFT **Having an idea for a painting, the author made a preliminary sketch in pastel of the view through the window. The pale blue sky is echoed in the stronger blue of the right-hand door. By contrast, the warm, pale tints on the lefthand door reflect the sunlight.**

LEFT **Fishing boats beached at Hastings were the inspiration for this rapid pen sketch.**

Graphite pencils are available in a wide range from very hard to very soft. The soft range 2B to 6B is suitable for sketching. The softer the lead, the broader the mark you can make. It is best to keep your pencils sharpened roughly to a point so that it is possible to vary the line from thin to thick by changing the angle at which you hold the pencil. The technique generally used is crosshatching.

RIGHT This charcoal sketch was executed by the author in under 10 minutes. He then had to flee the driving wind and rain!

ABOVE **Planes of light and dark tone in the hillside houses were the inspiration for this study. The author used a 3b pencil.**

ABOVE The spherical shape of these trees make a suitable subject for pencil crosshatching.

ABOVE The author used a soft pencil for this drawing.

CROSSHATCHING

The drawing is made by a build-up of short lines placed at a regular angle across the paper. The angle of the pencil is then changed and the lines crossed again. This process continues until the drawing is "complete." Alternatively, the initial sketch can be made with a very soft pencil, after which the lines are "smudged" with the finger to move the tone around and create areas of light and dark.

The same technique may be used with charcoal. Again, this medium is produced in hard and soft form, both as a pencil and in sticks. Charcoal is ideal for "smudging," where large areas of tone can be created very quickly.

HARVEST, NEAR DATCHWORTH, HERTFORDSHIRE

ENID FAIRHEAD

Enid Fairhead is from the tradition of *en plein air* painters. She searches for her motifs and, when she has found inspiration, works directly on the spot and without preliminary studies or drawings. She writes, "I am fortunate to live in the midst of lovely English countryside – the source of my inspiration as a landscape painter. Visually, one of the most exciting times for me is the harvest – seas of vibrant tawny golds, bleached grasses, and bright greens giving way to blue purple and bronzed greens."

Author's Notes

What fascinates this artist about this view is the way the lines of wheat and stubble converge at the large trees in the middle distance. This makes for a natural focal point, which she is careful to place slightly off-center. She is intimately concerned with light and its effects on color, which changes according to the time of day. "It is always better to paint landscape up to mid-morning and from mid-afternoon, when the shadows are angled, accentuating form. This can disappear in the flattening noon light."

Enid normally prefers to work on a colored ground, because this provides a key for color and tonal unity at the start. She uses well-diluted paint to apply glazes across the picture, gradually using her paint more thickly with each glaze. She never completely covers the preceding layer, but allows tints of translucent color beneath to remain and contribute to the overall subtlety.

Materials

Paints: Titanium white, lemon yellow, cadmium yellow, yellow ocher, raw sienna, cadmium orange, light red, alizarin crimson, and ultramarine.

Brushes: Size No. 5, 6, and 7 bristle filberts and No. 4 pointed sable.

Support: Masonite primed with three coats of acrylic white primer.

1 A quick charcoal sketch of the scene.

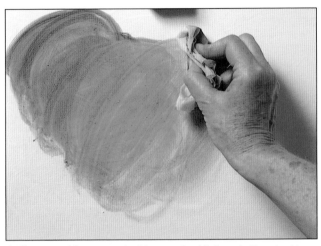

2 The ground is prepared with a wash of light red diluted with turpentine.

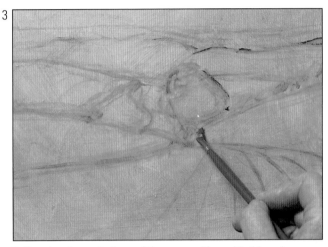

3 Drawing the main lines of the composition with thinned raw sienna. A No. 4 filbert bristle brush is used for this.

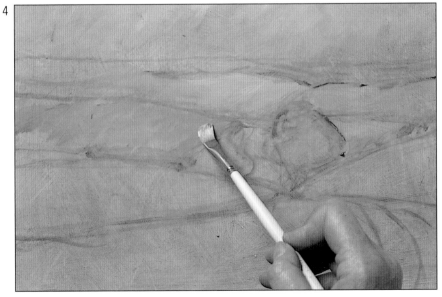

4 Patches of color, ultramarine mixed with white and a little crimson, are worked into the sky with a No. 6 flat-bristle brush. Yellow ocher, cadmium orange, raw sienna, and light red are brushed into the fields, using turpentine only.

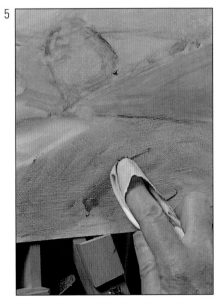

5 The artist occasionally rubs in color with a rag to spread the tones more quickly.

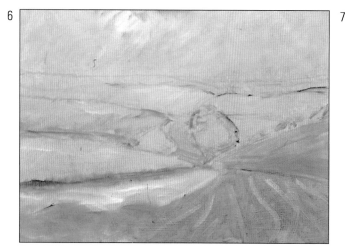

6 The first glaze of warm tints is complete.

7 Ultramarine and raw sienna are mixed to make a cool green to mark the trees. The horizon line is indicated with a mix of ultramarine and lemon yellow, then rubbed down with a cloth.

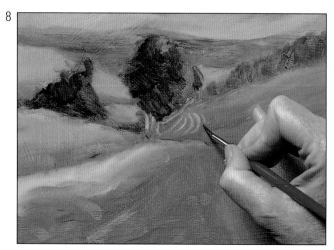

8 Thicker glazes are now being used, following the "fat over lean" principle. Furrow lines are drawn into the mid-distance field with a pointed sable brush dipped in turpentine.

9 A No. 4 bristle brush is well loaded to paint a mix of thick yellow ocher and white for the bright grain tops.

10 The corn stubble lines are drawn in using the edge of a flat bristle brush.

11 A No. 2 pointed bristle brush is employed to touch in the tractor with a mixture of cadmium orange and light red.

12 A mix of thick pale yellow is applied to the tops of the wheat, increasing contrast and introducing more texture.

13 The painting is almost finished, and the artist decides that some final touches of blue and pink are needed in the sky.

14 More touches of violet and blue are scumbled in the distant horizon to add more atmospheric perspective.

15 The finished painting.

PEN SKETCHING

Any type of pen (and there are many) can be used for sketching. Keep a felt tip or ballpoint pen handy for making quick notes. Ink cartridge sketching pens are a good investment, because you do not have to carry bottles of ink around with you. They can produce a variable thickness of line similar to a dipping pen. Using water-soluble ink enables you to produce tone as well as line, simply by moistening parts of the drawing and then spreading the ink with your finger. Many artists still prefer the dip pen, because of its quality of line and the fact that tonal areas and texture can be created by dipping tissue paper or a sponge into the bottle.

All the sketches on this spread were done by the author. The pens used are different in each case. They were selected to suit the subject and the type of study being attempted.

OPPOSITE TOP **A fairly quick cross-hatched study of a copse of trees focuses on structure, form, and tone. A felt-tip pen was used.**

OPPOSITE BELOW **Here, interest lies in the relationship between the geometric shapes of the buildings set against the textural masses of the trees. Line combined with crosshatched fountain pen was the method used.**

ABOVE **Cypress trees set against the spherical-shaped tree in the center provide the visual interest in this dip-pen sketch.**

LEFT **This ballpoint pen sketch of a stream running through woodland is the first study for a future painting.**

BRUSH DRAWING

Sketching with a brush dipped in paint or ink can produce delightful effects. Rembrandt and Constable were masters in its use, when they wanted to catch the effects of large, contrasting areas of light and dark. If you are prepared to carry the necessary equipment – brushes, a palette, some paint, and cloths – it is possible to produce dramatic tonal drawings quite quickly.

RIGHT **Fishing boats in Hastings, by the author. A rapid sketch in acrylic color on prepared paper.**

BELOW **The author made this watercolor study overlooking an inlet on the Cornish coast. Both wet-in-wet and wet-on-dry techniques were used.**

ABOVE The center of interest for the author in this scene is the surf breaking on the rocks. Watercolor heightened with white gouache (for the surf) has been used.

ABOVE Both these brush and ink sketches by the author are of the same scene. They are the first studies for a painting. The sketch on the left zooms in closer to the couple on the bench so less background is included than in the sketch on the right.

ABBEY VIEW

T E D   G O U L D

This mural is now instaled in the foyer of a development in Watford, Hertfordshire. It was produced in the studio and is the culmination of several studies done on location during the Fall.

Author's Notes

The title *Abbey View* is also the name of the high-rise building where the mural now hangs and is the r*aison d'être* of the picture. From the top of the tower it is just possible to see the tower of St. Albans Abbey projecting above a line of trees, about 8 miles distant. It was obviously not feasible to work so far away from the subject, so I made a trip to St. Albans to seek out a much closer position. I discovered that the view across the lake in front of the abbey is quite delightful and offered all the elements for color and composition that I could desire. I immediately sat down to make a watercolor study and also take some photographs. The next task was to return to my studio and collect everything that would be necessary for at least two days' painting outdoors.

When working far from my means of transportation, I find that a shopping cart suits my needs perfectly. All the materials are contained either inside the bag or strapped to the outside, and the whole ensemble fits easily into the trunk and the wheels of the cart are robust enough to cope with fairly rough terrain.

The kit I take for an oil-painting expedition includes: a portable easel; a paintbox with compartments for brushes, palette, and solvents; a collapsible chair; a sun umbrella; a viewfinder; sketchbooks; and some rags for brush and palette cleaning. I also pack a guy rope with a couple of tent pegs to hold the easel down in windy conditions. A flask of hot coffee is a must!

An important consideration is clothing. Even when the weather looks nice, it can change. It may feel warm when walking, but having to keep still for a couple of hours can make you more susceptible to the slightest breeze. So I normally take a hat, warm jacket, and sweater, thick socks, and strong shoes — even, on occasion, gloves!

Materials
Paints: Venetian red, cadmium red, cadmium yellow medium, lemon yellow, yellow ocher, oxide of chromium green, cobalt blue, cerulean blue, blue violet, black, titanium white.
Support: Canvas board.
Brushes: No. 2, 5, 6, and 8 filbert bristle, No. 2 pointed sable, No. 4 flat sable.

1 Photograph of St. Albans Abbey seen across the lake.

2 Watercolor study done on the spot.

3 Traveling to the painting location with my "kit."

4 Before unpacking and setting up the easel, etc., I use the viewfinder to survey the scene and find the best position.

5 Set up and making a start. The picture is drawn with charcoal, and the viewfinder is used to find the positions and directions of the main composition lines.

6 I continue to draw. The sun umbrella is now up, shading the white support from strong sunlight.

7 The palette and the detachable palette rest. The solvent containers are also detachable from the palette, but I like to keep them close to the color. One contains pure turpentine, the other a linseed oil and turpentine mix.

8

8 The first washes of color being applied: cerulean blue with a little white for the sky, cadmium yellow and violet for the screen of autumn trees. A No. 7 filbert bristle brush is used.

9

10

9 The completed painting. Separate studies were made of the swans, which were added later in the studio. The painting has been done in exactly the same proportion as the intended mural – that is, it is exactly the same shape, but much smaller.

The next stage is to "scale up" the painting to the same size as the larger mural. The support for the mural is cotton canvas, stretched over a wood frame and primed with acrylic white. The size of the mural is 6 × 7 feet.

Scaling-up was achieved by drawing a grid of squares onto tracing paper and laying this over the painting. Exactly the same number of squares was drawn onto the mural support using charcoal. It was then possible to draw the basic composition onto the mural support, using the squares overlaying the painting as reference points.

10 The finished mural painting.

11

11 Detail of the mural.

PHOTO-SKETCHING

The use of the camera as an aid to painting is still the subject of debate. Many artists feel that photography is a different medium altogether and its use by painters leads directly to mere copying and the loss of drawing skills. However, the photograph has been used by artists for almost a hundred years. Any medium that a painter uses or borrows from has its own intrinsic qualities, which can change the character of the work. Edgar Degas, the Impressionist painter, made extensive use of the photograph, which opened up new possibilities in composition for him.

One advantage of the modern camera loaded with high-speed film is that it is now possible to record forms in motion: the running figure, a racehorse, etc. For the landscape artist, skilful use of the camera can

provide a very useful reference source of complex details that would take hours to draw.

ABOVE AND BELOW **The author discovered this scene while looking for subjects to paint. Two overlapping photographs were taken to act as reference for the oil painting below.**

GARDEN LANDSCAPE

KAY GALLWEY

Kay Gallwey does not use the traditional pastel painter's method of "layering." That is to say that she does not "block in" areas of color and then work over and into them. She prefers bold strokes of color, using the thin edge of the pastel. For her it is essential to stay in touch with the ground, never entirely covering it.

Author's Notes

This picture, vibrant with color and movement, was not done on location, but was produced from a magazine cutout that took the artist's eye. No preliminary studies were made – the painting is entirely spontaneous and executed on the spot.. The artist works fast, continually standing well back from the painting, so that she can assess the progress of the whole. Long strokes of color appear right across the picture to start with. She does not "dally" in any particular area and when changing to another color continues to use it, finding the right places for it all over the picture.

The work progresses by adding more lines, occasionally smudging an area to prevent it from becoming dominant, introducing a pink here to add richness and a more neutral violet there to unify areas of color. Finally, Kay puts in some touches of fluorescent pastel, to give the painting its ultimate brilliance.

Materials

Pastels: Cerulean blue, sky blue, cobalt blue, ultramarine blue, pale violet, turquoise blue, pink, orange, red, lemon yellow, chrome green, oxide green deep, purple, and black.

Fluorescent Pastels: Pink, orange, and green.

Support: 100 pound NOT tinted cover paper.

1 A spread from a garden magazine was the inspiration for the painting.

2 The artist does not start with a neutral base drawing. She launches straight into the picture, placing patches and flicks of color right across the surface.

3 Broad strokes of yellow with the pastel held lengthwise indicate the field and sunlit foliage.

4 Light green is applied in rapid strokes around the painting, changing to a complementary pink and light blue.

5 Touches of white are added to keep the color key light.

6 Strokes of dark green are added to some areas in shadow, gradually increasing the contrast with the light pinks and blues of the flowers.

7 Black is employed here to provide a link between the surrounding contrasting tones.

8 More pink is applied to the flowers progressively, making the picture more dense and saturated with color. Note that the artist never completely covers the background paper with solid color.

9 Dark blue is added to the green of the foliage to increase contrast with the yellow bushes in front.

10 Gently rubbing the pastel in the background bushes softens the forms and increases the sense of atmospheric perspective.

11 To increase the contrast between foreground and background, dark violet is applied between the bright tones. This also has the effect of creating more spatial depth to the picture surface.

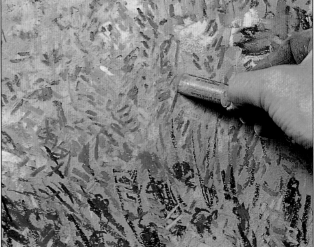

12 Touches of fluorescent pastel have been placed in the flowers and foreground foliage. This gives the picture a little more "sparkle." The painting is nearly complete, and the artist considers the finishing touches.

13 A few more strokes of blue to the central part of the painting and some touches of violet create more spatial depth.

14 The finished painting.

4
COLOR AND LIGHT

Color and light are inseparable elements in all painting. We cannot see color without light, and the color of light itself affects all the local colors in our field of vision.

A peculiarity of landscape painting, and an essential consideration for the artist, is the effect on color caused by the atmosphere. This is negligible when painting portraits or still lives but, where distance is involved, the atmosphere will make a radical difference to the color and tone of an object. For example, a house near the horizon will appear light and grayish, almost disappearing on a misty day, by comparison with a similar building in the foreground.

COLOR THEORY

There are only three basic colors – red, blue, and yellow. From these three primary colors, all the other colors are mixed. This sometimes comes as an astonishing fact to those just starting out as painters.

Secondary colors are obtained by mixing the primaries in equal quantities.

Tertiary colors are obtained by mixing different quantities of the primaries together:

2 parts yellow with 1 part red	=	yellow/orange
2 parts red with 1 part yellow	=	red/orange
2 parts blue with 1 part yellow	=	blue/green
1 part yellow with 2 parts blue	=	green/blue

Of course, the theory is based on the colors that are produced by light. In painting we use colors that are found in the earth or are manufactured in a chemical laboratory.

ABOVE **Painting color triangles like this one is a good way of learning the different mixtures that can be obtained from the three primary colors, red, blue, and yellow. These, which cannot be mixed from any other colors, are placed one at each corner. The first inner triangle shows the secondary colors, mixed from any pair of primaries, while within this are the tertiaries, the neutral colors mixed from the secondaries. This triangle shows cobalt blue, cadmium yellow, and alizarin crimson, but you can vary the primary hues, which will give a different set of mixtures.**

VISCOSITY

The degree to which paint is diluted is important for different working situations and the various stages of a painting. Like the Impressionists, most location painters use heavily diluted paint to assist them to work quickly. The "fat over lean" principle (thicker paint applied over thinner) means that less diluent is used the further a painting progresses, until areas of impasto (straight from the tube) are used in the final stages.

A graphic demonstration of the use of primary color is in front of you as you read this book. All the color illustrations have been printed using only the three printing primaries – magenta, cyan blue, and yellow – plus black for definition. The mass of different tones are achieved by printing tiny dots of pure color alongside each other.

DIRECTION OF LIGHT

Apart from the color of light, the other important factor in landscape painting is the direction of light. There are four directions from which light can illuminate a scene: front, side, back, and top. On cloudy, overcast days, the direction is usually from above. The tops of objects are the lightest, casting a pool of soft shadow beneath. The absence of sunlight reduces contrast both in color and tone, producing a generally muted effect.

TOP LEFT Backlighting occurs at the extreme ends of the day, at dawn and at sundown. In this case, the light is coming directly toward the painter from low in the sky. The sky itself is the brightest area in the scene, reducing all the objects between the sky and the artist to silhouettes, with long vertical shadows in front. In this study the girl carrying the basket has fine highlights on her head, the side of her basket, and the edge of her blouse.

LEFT Side lighting. This study assumes that the light is coming from the left and fairly low down. The sun is bright in a cloudless sky, causing the trees, figure, and building to be seen three-dimensionally and in sharp relief. Shadows are cast diagonally from the right side of the objects. Strong side lighting illustrates Cézanne's thesis that all nature is based on the sphere, cone, and cylinder.

BELOW LEFT Front lighting. The position of the sun is directly behind the artist in this study. The effect is to increase the color temperature to its warmest and flatten the shapes of everything. The angle of the light source is high, so that the shadows are underneath the forms.

Using the landscape study described in these exercises, do three studies of your own in acrylic or oil demonstrating the points made in the text.

Color temperature

We tend to think of color as either warm or cool with reds and yellows at the warm end of the spectrum, blues and violets at the cool end. Colors themselves can be made warmer or cooler in mixing. For example: red mixed with very little blue becomes cool red; green mixed with more yellow becomes warm green.

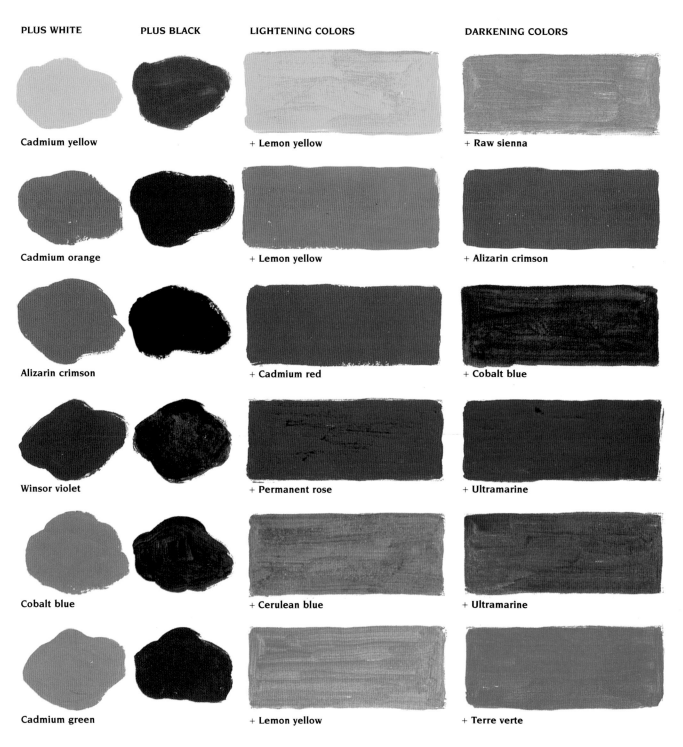

PLUS WHITE	PLUS BLACK	LIGHTENING COLORS	DARKENING COLORS
Cadmium yellow		+ Lemon yellow	+ Raw sienna
Cadmium orange		+ Lemon yellow	+ Alizarin crimson
Alizarin crimson		+ Cadmium red	+ Cobalt blue
Winsor violet		+ Permanent rose	+ Ultramarine
Cobalt blue		+ Cerulean blue	+ Ultramarine
Cadmium green		+ Lemon yellow	+ Terre verte

Neutral tones

These can be described as warm, or cool grays. In painting, neutrals can be mixed from the primary and secondary colors laid out on your palette; for instance, orange mixed with blue and broken with a little white, will produce a medium gray. Payne's Grey can be described as a medium gray that can be made warmer or cooler by the addition of Red or Blue.

Neutral tones are very important as a link or a division between pure, brilliant colors, particularly in landscape painting. They also have the effect of unifying the whole composition.

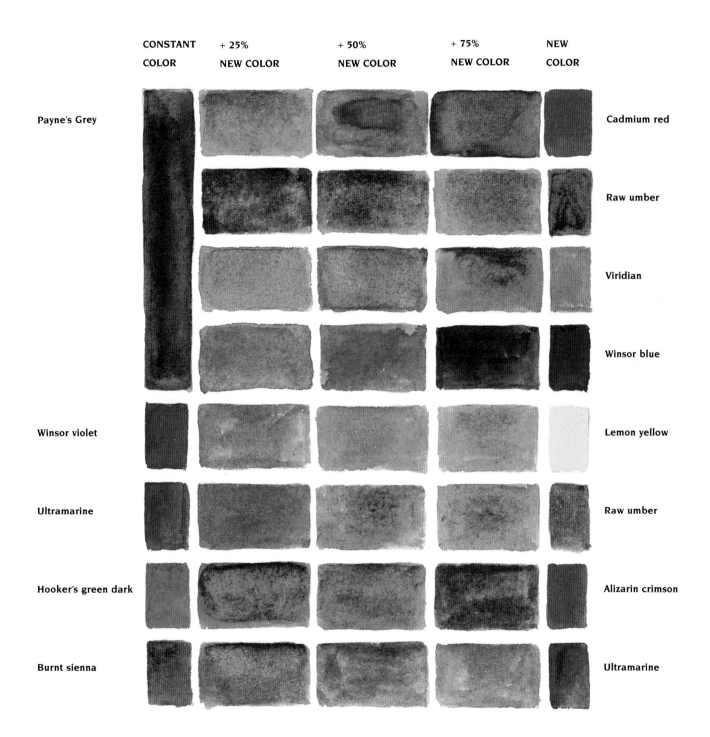

	CONSTANT COLOR	+ 25% NEW COLOR	+ 50% NEW COLOR	+ 75% NEW COLOR	NEW COLOR	
Payne's Grey						Cadmium red
						Raw umber
						Viridian
						Winsor blue
Winsor violet						Lemon yellow
Ultramarine						Raw umber
Hooker's green dark						Alizarin crimson
Burnt sienna						Ultramarine

BOY MEETS OCEAN

KENNETH SWAIN

The boy is the artist's son Jonathan. This oil painting is not the result of hours spent on location working in front of the subject. Although it is hard to believe that a picture so full of light, color, and atmosphere was not painted on the spot, it was actually done from start to finish in the studio.

Author's Notes

The idea for the painting came several weeks after the event when Ken saw a photograph taken while he was introducing his son to the water. This gray, monochrome image was enough to activate the color sensations that had been stored in his mind through acute observation.

There are no preliminary studies or drawings made. The artist has launched directly into the full-size painting, making a simple charcoal sketch first and then applying patches of dry color into the sky and water. The color areas are rubbed down, repainted, and generally modified until they approximate to the image in his mind. In fact, there are only two main

stages to this work. The first, as described above, continues using dryish color, until all the forms are balanced against each other across the entire painting. The second stage is impasto. The artist employs a palette knife, a penknife, and a small bristle brush to apply modeling and texture to the underpainting.

Materials

Paints: Magenta, alizarin crimson, Prussian blue, Payne's grey, burnt and raw umber, yellow ocher, cadmium red, cadmium yellow, cadmium orange, chrome green, chrome green deep, cerulean blue, lemon yellow, and Indian yellow.
Brushes: Bristle brushes No. 4 to 10.
Penknife and palette knife.
Support: Primed canvas.

1 This monochrome photograph served as the only reference for this picture.

2 The artist begins with a light charcoal drawing outlining the main color and tonal areas. A touch of diluted flesh color is used to position the figure. No base color has been applied, because the intention is to use high-key, pure color throughout this painting.

3 The color of the sky will set the key for the entire picture. Washes of Prussian blue broken with a little white and black are brushed in, using a No. 10 flat-bristle brush.

4 Pinkish tints are added near the horizon line. The Prussian blue is used in the sea, reflecting the color of the sky and then broken with lemon yellow to produce a translucent green. The color is used thin and "rubbed" into the white canvas.

5 Patches of diluted color are now placed all around the painting following the principle that a picture should look somewhat finished at every stage. Yellow ocher, crimson, cadmium red, and burnt umber are added to the palette. They are mixed and still used *thinly* to establish the waves and rock shapes. Bristle brushes sizes 4 and 10 are used. The artist uses a cloth to rub down certain areas.

7 Mixing darker tones of Prussian blue and burnt umber. The rock forms are stressed and divided into sharper planes of color.

8 The sky area has been modulated with thicker paint using tones of pink, blue, and yellow. The child's torso is more finely washed with warm tints of orange.

6 From now on, the palette knife is brought into use to apply thick color, which is then "scratched and scraped" back with the tip of a penknife. The child's figure represents the focal point of the painting, so the artist builds up the color here first. Similar warm tints of yellow ocher and red are then "found" in the rocks, reflections in the water, and the sky.

9 White is worked into the sea forms and to the surf, to soften and "feather" the color. A No. 4 round bristle brush is used with the palette knife to create texture.

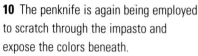

10 The penknife is again being employed to scratch through the impasto and expose the colors beneath.

11 Adding more tones of pure color. Chrome orange is used here with the palette knife to create the skin tones reflected in the water. Burnt umber is worked into the child's figure and the rocks to stress form. Colors are now used straight from the tube without first being mixed or diluted.

12 The picture is nearly finished, and it is time to take stock and decide where the final touches and alterations should be made.

13 A little more impasto white, occasionally broken with tints of blue, green, and pink, is applied to increase the sense of atmosphere and light.

14 The finished painting.

USING COLOR

Painters always strive to reproduce the effects of light on color in landscape. Only an approximation can be achieved with paint, which, after all is simply a pigment suspended in a binder. The colors in a scene on a wintry, misty day will generally be at the cool end of the spectrum. On a clear, sunny day, the same scene will be dominated by colors toward the warm end.

RIGHT AND BELOW Two oil studies employing cool and warm palettes:
RIGHT Prussian blue, violet, burnt umber and yellow ochre.
BELOW Venetian red, orange, cadmium yellow and chrome green.

OLIVE TREES WITH DONKEY

TED GOULD

The idea for this oil painting came as the result of a short trip to Crete during early summer. As usual, I had a small sketchbook with some tubes of gouache and my camera. We came across an area of the island that was given over to grain fields and olive trees, interspersed with the occasional melon grove. Here and there, I could see a donkey sheltering from the midday sun. The scene was made even more attractive by a range of mountains running behind the fields and parallel to the horizon. I sat down right away to make a quick study and to take some photographs.

Author's Notes

There are two dominant color complementaries running throughout this landscape: yellow and blue/green, which create something of a counterchange pattern. The whole is held together by the bright cerulean blue of the sky and the blue/violet of the mountains.

After the underpainting is completed, areas of thicker, more textural paint are applied using a knife. The term palette knife properly applies to those with long handles used for mixing paint on the palette. Painting knives have short broad blades with "cranked" handles to keep the hand out of the wet paint. They feel flexible and springy, and produce a variety of effects, always wonderfully spontaneous and bold. There is almost a sense of modeling the paint onto the canvas. Light is reflected off the strokes and textures, keeping the surface lively.

Dragging the knife at an angle with firm pressure spreads the paint in a transparent layer with thick "edges," rather in the manner of spreading soft butter on bread. Using the point with short, sharp patting movements produces a raised texture of points. Fine lines can be drawn while simultaneously turning the knife to score through the surface layers in a sgraffito effect.

Materials

Paints: Cerulean blue, ultramarine blue, mauve, Indian red, chrome green or light oxide green, winsor yellow, yellow ocher, titanium white, and lamp black.

Brushes: No. 3 and 5 hog bristles, flat and filbert.

Palette knives: Large and small, pointed.

Support: Primed canvas board.

1 A photograph of the area.

2 A base drawing in charcoal and yellow ocher diluted with turpentine is the first stage. This places the shapes in space and indicates the main composition lines.

3 Beginning the underpainting. The intention is to paint the entire picture with thinly diluted paint first, then when dry, to work over the top using palette knives. Starting at the top with cerulean blue, mauve, and chrome green, the sky, mountains, and foreground tree are brushed in lightly. A No. 5 filbert bristle brush is used.

4 The figure and donkey are brushed in using a mix of mauve and yellow. Parts of the drawing are lost during this process and then restored by drawing back with ultramarine and mauve.

5 Yellow ocher and Indian yellow are mixed for the grain fields, which are painted as a flat wash. A No. 5 filbert bristle brush is used.

6 The underpainting is complete. A soft cloth has been used to rub down wet areas and spread the color. The painting is left to dry for a few hours.

7 The palette knife painting is begun by mixing cerulean blue with a little white and a touch of linseed oil, working broadly across the sky using a large pointed knife.

8 The mountains are indicated with mauve and ultramarine added to the cerulean. This is broken with white and a touch of yellow ocher toward the base, which creates a heat-haze effect.

9 Tree foliage is painted with a mix of chrome green and ultramarine, keeping the knife well loaded with color and changing the angle continually to create texture.

10 The tip and edge of the knife are employed to put in the cypress trees in the background.

11 A good thick mix of yellow ocher, Indian red, and a touch of mauve is applied to the grain fields. The knife is turned regularly and used to scratch and scrape back to reveal the underpainting.

12 Modulating the colors in the middle ground.

13 A small pointed palette knife is used to model the foreground tree foliage and to create texture.

14 Black is added to the deep shadow areas such as tree branches. Final touches of Indian red and mauve are mixed to add texture to the grasses and shadow areas under the trees.

15 The finished picture.

FISHING BOATS

T E D   G O U L D

This study of fishing boats in a Portuguese harbor is the result of a brief visit to a little harbor in the Algarve region. The fishermen were repairing their nets in preparation for the next day, and they were all busy in their brightly colored boats.

Author's Notes

Standing on the dock, I took some photographs before moving on to the next stop on the journey. When I saw the prints later, I was reminded of the vibrating image of reflected light and decided to make a bleach drawing to attempt to recreate the sensation.

Materials

Watercolor board (NOT), a flat sable brush, household bleach, black fountain-pen ink, a dipping pen, white conté pencil, cotton-wool swabs and a child-safe container for the bleach.

Note: bleach is caustic and must be kept well away from children. *Do not allow any skin contact*. Also, do not use sable or bristle brushes with bleach as it will quickly rot the hairs.

1 The photograph that provided the reference for the drawing.

2 Watercolor board is covered with a good wash of ink using a flat sable brush. When this has dried thoroughly, the composition is sketched in with conté pencil.

3 Starting with a cotton swab dipped in bleach, the light areas are etched back. Only a little bleach is used at first, because if the swab is too heavily loaded, it will clean the ink off right down to the board's surface.

4 The swab is used all over the light areas, gradually applying more bleach to increase the contrast between light and dark.

5 Finally a pen dipped in bleach is employed to draw in the details and highlights.

Color used to unify a painting

As already stated, neutral colors have the effect of creating unity. Adopting a limited palette of colors close together on the spectrum is an aid to achieving a unity of the whole picture. It is also advisable for those just starting to paint.

R I G H T **Smooth washes of color in this seascape by Robert Tilling give an impression of great space and depth. A limited palette of three or four colors has been used with strong tonal contrasts providing the visual interest.**

Using a bright complementary as a focal point

Bring out a point of particular interest in a picture by using a complementary color in contrast to the general color scheme.

R I G H T **A rapid oil study by the author done while on vacation in Dorset. The inspiration for the picture was the backdrop of the dark, ominous sky set against the warm sandstone church tower. The red boat anchored in front of the church provides a strong focal point.**

Contrasting high-key color

Complementary colors can be used alongside each other when outlined, or separated by a neutral. Such color was the basis of the Fauvist movement and, of course, Van Gogh's work.

LEFT *Poplars*. **This acrylic by Gerry Baptist brilliantly exploits the complementaries pink, blue, and yellow to produce a vibrant painting full of light. The neutral black is cleverly used as a unifying factor. The composition counterpoints the verticals in the trees with the horizontal fields.**

BELOW *West Herts College*. **A gouache by the author which makes use of the primary colors blended together in washes of diluted color. A neutral gray with black lines encloses the central forms to make something of a frame for the composition.**

OASIS IN TUNISIA

T E D   G O U L D

A simple postcard which dropped through my mail box one morning is the basis for this picture. The distinctive shapes of the palm trees standing vertically on the rippled sand dunes make them a "natural" for the gouache lift technique

Author's Notes

I decided to use colored gouache to evoke the atmosphere of the desert. Three colors are used: cerulean blue, yellow ocher, and violet. The support is NOT surface watercolor board. Do not use a smooth surface paper or board because you will find that the textures are disappointing and the ink may lift off as well.

As can be seen, the gouache lift technique produces a similar effect to that achieved by a lino or wood cut. However, it is much quicker than either of those two methods, but, of course, you end up with just one original, whereas with lino or wood, you can make dozens of prints.

Materials

Paints: Violet, cerulean blue, and yellow ocher gouache color.

Brushes: No. 4 and 8 pointed sables.

No. 8 flat synthetic sable.

Ink: Waterproof India ink.

Support: NOT watercolor board.

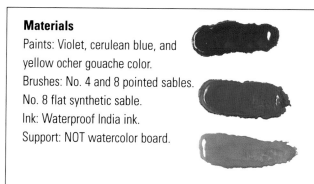

1 The postcard that inspired the picture.

2 A light pencil drawing is made onto the board. This defines the areas of light and dark and indicates the areas for painting in the gouache. Do not draw the lines too heavily; otherwise, they may be visible in the finished painting.

3 Full-strength color has been applied straight from the tube. Note that these colors will be lighter in tone when "washed off." Those areas where no ink is to penetrate have been painted thickly. The edges and some other parts have been dry brushed for texture. Remember that those parts left white will be black in the final picture. The paint should be left to dry completely. A No. 4 pointed sable brush was used.

4 The entire painting is now covered with an even layer of waterproof black ink, using a No. 8 pointed sable. The brush is well loaded with ink, which is applied as quickly as possible to avoid disturbing the gouache beneath. The ink layer must be left to dry completely before "washing off."

5 The final "washing off" stage is best done under a slow-running cold faucet. The gouache slowly dissolves and lifts the ink off the painted areas. This process is assisted by gently rubbing with a large sable brush until all the surface gouache has been removed.

6 The finished picture.

TREES AT Ste. FOY
(BORDEAUX REGION)

G E R R Y   B A P T I S T

Gerry Baptist likes to travel, particularly in the warm Mediterranean climate
– not for him the cool greens and dark grays of the English landscape.
He acknowledges the influence of the Fauves on his color, but the expressive
power of this acrylic painting contains echoes of the German "Blaue Reiter"
group.

Author's Notes

A quick comparison of the painting with its reference demonstrates the fact that the photograph has been used as little more than a starting point for the picture. The scene was originally glimpsed from a car window as the artist was traveling through the area, resulting in the photograph on page 90.

Before starting the final painting, various studies are made exploring different color schemes. These are important in the process of translating the greens and grays in the photograph to the bright sensuous colors used in the picture.

The artist likes to establish bright, contrasting base colors for his pictures. They function as the color key for the entire work. In this painting there are three complementary base colors. He then draws the main forms and lines of the composition and expands the shapes with thicker paint. Further planes of color are applied, usually complementaries of the one beneath. More glazes are overlaid as the picture grows and changes, often leaving some of the underlying colors "exposed." In addition to glazing, he "feathers" some of the layers one into the other to create gently receding or advancing planes, The picture is "finished" when he feels that he cannot add anything more and the work appears to have its own independent existence.

Materials

Paints: Chrome yellow, chrome orange, chrome green, violet, emerald, pthalo green, pthalo blue, cerulean blue, acra red, magenta, black. Matte gel medium.
Brushes: Size No. 8 and 14 hog bristles and No. 8 synthetic sable.
Support: Fine cotton canvas primed with gesso.

1 The reference photograph which provides the starting point for the painting.

2 A preliminary study for the picture.

3 A base painting is prepared indicating broad horizontal areas of color, which the artist will continually modify throughout the painting. Emerald green, chrome orange, acra red, magenta, chrome green yellow, pthalo blue, and cerulean blue, are mixed and applied with a No. 14 bristle brush.

4 The base painting is complete and left to dry.

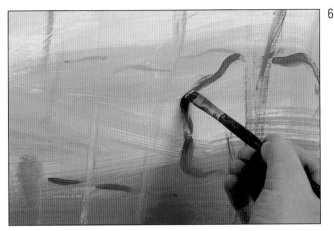

5 and **6** The foreground trees are brushed in with green, changing to violet mixed with white and red for the right-hand tree in the middle distance.

7 More dryish color has been brushed into the sky background and trees, which are worked alternately. Yellow, white, and cerulean blue are the principal colors used for this.

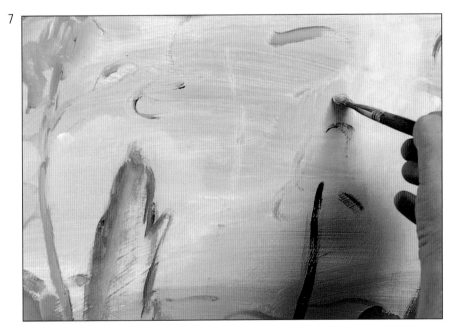

8 *Detail* Green tones are added to the foliage, contrasting with the violet in the trees behind.

9 More green is brushed into the foreground against the complementary pink. The whole picture is assessed by the artist at this stage.

10 Thicker pink is dry brushed onto blue, producing a violet fringe to the form. Matte gel medium is added to the colors at this stage to thicken them.

11

12

11 Some yellow is dry brushed and then feathered over the pink form. The artist moves from one area to another applying complementaries over previous colors.

12 This picture shows how the painting has changed by continually working different colors over the top of previous glazes. The paint is thick but dry, so that it can be scumbled onto the surface and feathered.

13 Forms in the foreground tree are built up with a blue and blue-green mix to pull them into the foreground. A No. 8 bristle brush is still being used.

13

14

14 The picture is nearly finished. More pale yellow has been brushed into the sky, and the tree foliage has been modulated with a little more pink and yellow.

15

15 The finished painting.

5

COMPOSITION

Painting is largely about the organization of shapes, colors, and lines in a satisfactory and pleasing manner. Composition is the difference between making a sketch and creating a picture, bringing order to apparent chaos. Some artists reconstruct from studies of the subject until they feel that all the elements of the picture are in harmony. Others, working on location, take time and great care to choose a view which fulfills all their needs for composition. In this the viewfinder is invaluable. Make one for yourself using mat board, black one side. You should make sure that the window is exactly the same proportion as the painting support being used.

When choosing a subject, and probably after a good deal of searching around, you sometimes find that the resulting painting is a disappointment. This is not simply that you cannot get down what you see, or that you have made the

wrong color choice. It is because the subject itself, although attractive, is not suitable for painting as it stands. When painting any aspect of nature, the artist is actually translating a three-dimensional subject into two

dimensions. Translation means interpretation, and this is precisely where composition studies are so important, because you are translating objects in space into lines, shapes, and colors on a flat rectangular plane.

PLANNING A PAINTING

When you are planning a painting, it is advisable to work to a small scale. The sketchbook is useful for

this. Do several studies for each subject – monochrome studies to work out the tonal contrasts and color studies to decide on your

final palette. When working out your studies, consider the points listed below.

ABOVE AND RIGHT This photograph of the river at Salisbury was taken with the aim of making an oil painting of the scene. The pencil study, by the author, made from the photograph compresses the image into a more compact, vertical composition. It also functions as a tonal analysis of the subject.

ABOVE AND RIGHT Both photograph and gouache sketch of olive trees were done on the spot by the author. The subject contains contrasts between the blue/green of the tree foliage and the yellow/brown of the fields. The photograph provides more details than can be achieved in a quick study.

Subject

For your first landscape, choose a view that is interesting without being too complex, one that contains both verticals (trees, buildings) and horizontals (fields, pathways, etc.).

RIGHT *Winfrith Newburgh*, **oil by the author. This is an example of a classically based composition. The trees set in the foreground represent verticals which form a contrast with the horizontal cottages behind. The green foliage of the trees also contrasts with the pinks and browns of the buildings.**

Contrast of scale

A contrast of scale adds impact and visual interest. You could place a large tree or rock in the foreground, a row of houses in the middle distance all against a backdrop of hills, or mountains in the background.

BELOW **The large tree in the foreground of this gouache study, by the author, cuts both top and bottom edges of the picture plane, increasing the sense of space and depth to the house in the middle distance.**

Diagonals

Angled shapes or lines add a sense of movement to a picture. They also function as a visual link between one part of a painting and another.

RIGHT **The figures in this gouache study by the author make a triangle with the apex at the top of the picture plane. They rest on a diamond-shaped cloth near an angled tree trunk. In fact, all the forms in this composition are placed at an angle to the edges of the picture; nothing is simply horizontal or vertical.**

BELOW **Several strong diagonals running parallel to each other emphasize the slope of the hillside on which this gouache study was made. The counterchange between light and dark areas creates a pattern which is bisected by the curving tree trunks going off the top of the picture plane.**

ROCKS ON THE ATLANTIC COAST

HAZEL SOAN

The artist discovered this beautiful stretch of coastline during one of her visits to South Africa. At the time she was not primarily concerned with a painting location, but with finding a suitable swimming spot for herself and her family. However, when she happened upon this series of inlets on the Cape Peninsula, she was inspired by what she saw, and set off immediately to explore the whole area for the most interesting views.

Author's Notes

The Cape Peninsula is on the Atlantic seaboard. It consists of a series of inlets interspersed with boulders and rocky outcrops, incised by coves of almost pure white sand. Much of this coastline is backed by high cliffs and a ridge of mountains in the background. A strong contrast is made between the rocks, piled up in many strange configurations and the smooth planes of sand cutting between them. This is the visual inspiration for the picture.

Hazel Soan uses a variety of watercolor techniques in this painting; wet-in-wet, wet-on-dry, glazing, masking, sponging, and waxing. She works intuitively, preferring to keep all her options open as the work progresses. As can be seen from this demonstration, she starts simply and broadly. A few light pencil marks are made to indicate key points in the composition and then light washes of color are added to establish the tonal areas. These are then textured, and further washes are laid in a progressive build-up to the finale.

1

2

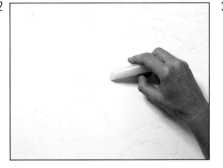

3

1 The main composition lines have been sketched in lightly with an HB pencil. Masking fluid is applied to the sketch to preserve the highlight areas all around the picture. A No. 3 pointed sable brush is used.

2 Candle wax is gently rubbed onto selected areas – particularly the rocks – to produce texture as the color washes are applied.

3 A broad wash of diluted yellow ocher covers most of the paper, except for the sky. This provides a warm key to the picture. A No. 14 pointed sable is used for this.

4

4 The sky area has been damped with clean water and diluted Prussian blue has been "touched in" to blend with the still-wet yellow ocher.

5 The blue has been brought down into the foreground rocks. Wax has been applied to the edge of the rock and yellow ocher is being washed over. The effect is to give a rough edge to the changing planes of color.

6 A little alizarin crimson has been added to the Prussian blue to create warmer cast shadows in the rocks.

7 The blue and violet areas are completed by "soaking off" some color toward the base of the mountains, thereby creating a misty effect.

8 Laying a glaze of slightly thicker yellow ocher over the rocks, making them warmer and defining their shape. "Spots" of alizarin crimson are dropped into the wet paint.

9 Deeper color is "dropped" into wet areas producing a "little explosion" effect. Wax is drawn into the rocks to protect previous washes and increase the textured effect. Alizarin crimson, yellow ocher, and Prussian blue are used.

9

10

10 A variety of techniques are now employed in painting the rocks – wet-in-wet, wet-on-dry, and wax. Darker tones of scarlet and blue are added to stress shape and color.

11

11 The broad washes are now completed, and the masking fluid is being removed with a kneaded eraser.

12 The complete picture so far.

13 Yellow ocher and Prussian blue are mixed to apply small wet-on-dry washes to the mountains and the rocks in the middle distance.

14 The artist has decided to modify a portion of the picture by taking out one of the rocks. Using a sable brush and clean water, she soaks off the color until it is almost obliterated and then retouches the area to leave it like the rest of the beach.

15

15 Pale Prussian blue is mixed to add ripples to the water and shadows around the middle-ground rock. A No. 7 pointed sable brush is used for this.

16

16 A natural sponge dipped in a mixture of Prussian blue and alizarin crimson is dabbed onto the foreground rocks to add surface texture.

17

17 The completed picture.

Light and dark

The balance of light and dark is a very important consideration. The dark or shadow areas of a picture set off the light, brightly colored areas. The one emphasizes the other and creates a sense of depth and contrast.

TOP AND MIDDLE **The trees in both these pastel sketches had deposited half their leaves on the ground. The visual sensation thus created was one of light yellow/brown contrasted with green/black.**

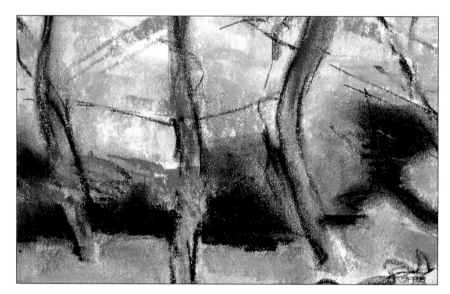

BELOW **Before starting a full-size painting, I frequently produce a tonal study of the subject, analyzing it in terms of light and dark. The importance of this is to establish a satisfactory composition for a fairly complex subject.**

Focal points

Some painters find it essential to create a clear focal point, or center of interest; others prefer to see their work as an overall pattern of shapes and colors, sometimes called architectural composition.

Two artists who saw composition as being of prime importance were Poussin and Cézanne. Both were acutely aware of the rectangular support in front of them and sought always to create a perfect balance within it – in the abstract sense. Let us aim for the same!

ABOVE A trawler sheltering in a bay off the Cornish coast prompted the author to attempt this watercolor study. The boat occupies a central position in the picture, leading the eye directly to it and creating a natural focal point. The distant hills behind provide a tonal link with the boat.

WHERE THE WATERS CROSS

TIMOTHY EASTON

This oil painting is of a view across a pond attached to a moat surrounding a country farmhouse. There are two islands to the left and right, and the sun rises on the left of the composition, creating some interesting shadows and highlights that help give distance across the water.

Author's Notes

During the warmer months of the year, there is usually a degree of certainty that successive days will be fine enough for a painting to progress outside. The artist finds that he can work on a number of canvases during a day, so the first session will start at 6.00 A.M., progress to 10.00 A.M., and the next will begin at 10.15 A.M. going on to the lunch break. This pattern can continue until 10.00 P.M. The paintings will be returned to for as many days as needed to complete each one. The canvas used here is double primed on linen, which is washed over with a medium-tone wash of color.

Materials

Paints: Titanium white, cadmium lemon, yellow ocher, Indian yellow, burnt sienna, burnt umber, cadmium red, permanent magenta, permanent sap green, olive green, cobalt blue, cerulean blue, French ultramarine.
Brushes: Hog hair sizes 1–5. Preferably filberts. Sable brushes finest quality No.7 (Winsor & Newton) short-handled.
Palette knife for pre-mixing only.

1

2

3

1 The initial view.

2 In the nuttery on the left-hand island is a flowering cherry tree, and it was anticipated that the picture would incorporate this, as well as the blossom that would come out a week later when the cherry blossom was over.

3 The canvas is covered with a base color of thinned olive green paint that allows both light and dark tones and color to register against a middle-toned color. *This base color must be totally dry before work begins.* The composition is then drawn in with a sable brush using thinned olive green paint.

4 Some broader areas of color are blocked in using a No. 3 hog's hair brush to give some idea of the balance of light and dark areas. No medium is used on the house and sky areas, but the color used on the water areas has been thinned out with turpentine.

5 The garden gateway is drawn in using a fine No. 2 sable brush and a mahlstick to steady the hand.

6 The sky and water areas are further established to give an overall impression of the light and dark masses. The sky is dry-brushed with some additional olive-green lines to suggest the form of the main tree branches.

7 The middle tone of the house roof reflected in the water is established using a No. 3 filbert hog's hair brush.

8

9

10

11

8 The colors along the top edge of the palette. Start with the light colors on the left: Yellows through to ochers, then to the reds: *mid-way* next to cadmium red are the complementary colors of sap and olive green, continuing on to blues. The colors below these are initially premixed using a palette knife. These two rows take up half the palette, leaving the other part free to be used for additional mixing as work progresses.

9 After one and a half hour's work, with the early morning sun creating strong contrasts in light and shade, the light areas are heightened to contrast with those in shadow.

10 The sky is further reworked using dry color, and into this the blossom of the flowering cherry tree is worked up using small dry dabs over the middle-tone areas of paint below. This detail shows the suggestion of the branches and leaves of the middle tree in the composition.

11 Adjustments are made to the color and proportions of the house, and the windows are added. There is a further reworking of the roof and blossom.

12 The light across the lawn showing between the gaps in the hedge is further heightened, and the water is also reworked, for greater contrast.

13 Having broadly established the tone, color, and contrast required, some smaller details are painted in using fine sable brushes.

14 Hog's hair brushes are used to define the water reflections.

15 A wind was driving the petals across the pond. The water is disturbed, and the arching of the petals helps to lead the eye across the pond from the bottom left-hand corner toward the bend in the moat.

16 More raking light is introduced into the part of the moat coming from the left, behind the nut trees and cherry.

16

17

17

17 The cherry blossom has now gone, but the may tree has fully flowered on the right side. The may blossom is added between young trees on the small island to the left of the picture. The chance arrival of the white duck offers a small detail in the foreground. Working on a picture over several days, with changing moods in the weather, means there are always incidents the artist can take advantage of. These "happenings" add interest to the composition. A painting done from a photograph captures only one moment in time, whereas a painting completed outdoors evolves over some time.

18

18 The finished picture. The top of the sky has been strengthened once more with a darker blue and some clouds introduced to reflect something of the light wind movement expressed in the arching petals on the surface of the pond.

Mt. ASPIRING

MARK TOPHAM

Mark Topham has chosen one of the classic landscape scenes for this gouache demonstration. Mountains framed by trees with a broad river meandering between verdant hills make for a challenging subject. The snow-capped mountains and sandbanks contrast sharply with the dark green water.

Author's Notes

The artist has a precise approach to his work. He takes time, before starting to do a visual analysis of the subject. He makes mental notes of the light and dark areas and the warm and cool colors he will need. He then indicates these areas on the support using a soft pencil. Choosing from a large range of colors, he assembles those he will need. Mark prefers to work with a greater number of pure colors, rather than mixing from a limited selection. His experience has given him the ability to work with and control more colors than would be recommended for a beginner.

The painting proceeds initially with diluted washes, leaving the very lightest areas white, until he has completed a delicate underpainting of the whole picture. He uses fairly small brush strokes, varying the tints as he goes. The process is then one of a gradual build-up of thicker paint, culminating in touches of white for highlights. The artist uses both the wet-in-wet and dry brush techniques, with some stipple and blotting for texture.

Materials

Paints: Permanent white, cadmium yellow, cadmium orange, raw umber, burnt sienna, raw sienna, burnt umber, azure blue, french ultramarine, indigo, viridian, spectrum violet, and acrylizing medium.

Brushes: Squirrel hair brush, No. 7 synthetic sable, No. 7 pointed sable.

Support: 140-pound NOT watercolor paper.

1 The painting is an interpretation of this photograph, which is the sole reference.

2 A base drawing of the main forms in this composition has been made using a 6B pencil. The sky is being washed in with a diluted mix of cerulean blue, ultramarine blue, and monastial blue. The paper has been slightly dampened, and the artist is pulling the wash down with a squirrel hair brush.

3 *Detail* Changing to a No. 7 synthetic sable brush, patches of color have been placed in the mountains using diluted pale violet. Green mixed with yellow ocher is being brushed into the middle-ground hills down to the shore line with the squirrel brush.

4 Thinned washes of blue with a little green are mixed for the water tones. Violet is added for the shadow areas. The artist has returned to the mountains, working with orange, white, burnt umber, and violet. The hills are lightened with white to create aerial perspective. This is done with a No. 7 pointed sable brush.

5

6

5 The first glazes are finished. Thicker paint will now be used mixed with some acrylizing medium to give body to the color.

6 The sky has been re-worked with blue and white to define the clouds. Darker shades of viridian green and raw sienna are mixed to paint the tree in shadow. More shades of dark green, blue, and raw sienna are used to finish the tree.

7

8

7 The picture looks one-sided at the moment – darker tones must be carried over to the middle hill on the right.

8 Texture in the right-hand hill is being applied with a No. 7 pointed sable brush. This is "feathered off" toward the horizon.

9 Still using the No. 7 sable brush, with a mix of green, blue, and raw sienna, the shadows and ripples are painted on the river.

10 Dryish color, a mix of light gray, has been brushed into the water to create reflections.

11 Now some light gray is dragged across the snow and rocks with the finger.

12 White with a little pink, used thickly, is applied to the banks and to suggest snow floating in the water. Some white is scumbled onto the foreground to indicate ripples.

13 Final touches for highlights are added to the tree, and the painting is finished.

14 The picture represents a beautiful study of the cool atmospheric effects of this region.

PERSPECTIVE

Perspective is the means by which an artist can create the illusion of depth in a painting. It is an important aid to the landscape painter, although it should not be allowed to displace the principles of good composition. There has been an awareness of these principles since the time of ancient Egypt, but were not fully developed until the Italian Renaissance, when Paolo Uccello and Leonardo da Vinci became interested in the theory of, and made extensive use of, perspective.

ABOVE A splendid example of single-point perspective is provided by Paolo Ucello's *The Rout of San Romano* (1397–1475). The direction of the fallen lances indicates a fairly high eye level, with the vanishing point near the center.

BELOW This drawing by Leonardo da Vinci shows the grid system he developed on which to construct his perspectives.

Main principles

If you stand looking out through an upstairs window, the point directly in line with your vision is the eye level. The window frame in front of you is your canvas or picture plane. In single-point perspective, the point on the eye level, straight ahead is the vanishing point (see fig. 1), where all lines parallel to your line of vision will converge. This is known as linear perspective.

Aerial perspective concerns color and tone, and is governed by the effects of light and atmosphere. We realize that hills and trees in the far distance are indistinct and light in tone, whereas a tree that is close up in the foreground is sharply focused with rich, contrasting color.

I have illustrated here the four main situations in which the painter will need to have a knowledge of perspective. They are: one-point, (high and low eye levels), two-point, and three-point perspective. Note what a radical difference the position of the eye level makes to the same scene.

ABOVE **Single-point, low eye level.**

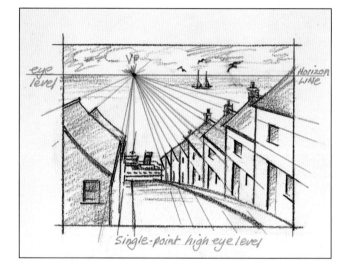

ABOVE **Single-point, high eye level.**

ABOVE **Two-point, low eye level.**

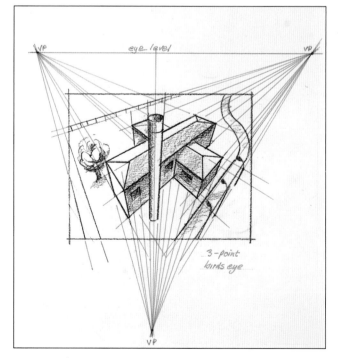

ABOVE **Three-point, bird's-eye view.**

ABOVE *Cornfields and Roses*. This oil by Timothy Easton is a *tour de force* of landscape painting. His delicate, sure brushwork combines with an unerring sense of tone and color which results in an immensely accomplished picture.

OLD FISHGUARD, PEMBROKESHIRE

MIKE BERNARD

Mike Bernard is absorbed by the tactile experience of working with a variety of materials. His main concerns are with the picture surface and the textures he produces. He delights in the discovery of unexpected effects obtained by the random use of materials and gains satisfaction when a "happy accident" occurs.

Author's Notes

He prefers not to have detailed references of the subject or to work on location, because too much visual information inhibits his creative response to the subject. For this painting, his only reference is the outline pencil sketch of the harbor and a photograph providing a glimpse of the scene.

His materials are chosen for their variety, offering the possibility for the unexpected to happen. Nevertheless, this is still a "controlled" process. The artist is fully aware of the nature of these diverse ingredients and what is likely to happen when they are combined.

The painting process begins with rough cut-outs of different papers

mounted on the support. Waterproof inks are then applied and allowed to run into each other to form other colors and textures. Successive layers of ink, paper, and paint are created, eventually producing the rich, dense final picture.

Materials

Inks: Orange, blue, black.
Pastels: Orange, pink, violet, pale green, blue, brown.
Acrylic: White and acrylic matte medium.
Papers: Various, including tissue and newsprint.

Support: 90-pound Hot Pressed watercolor paper.
Equipment: 1-inch varnish brush, flat and pointed synthetic sable brushes, small printing roller, dipping pens, a toothbrush, a pointed palette knife, and scissors.

1 The artist is much more concerned with luminous color, surface texture, and good formal structure than with straightforward representation, so he prefers the simplest of reference material. In this case it consists of a line sketch and a photograph providing some detail of the foreground boat.

2 Strips of paper, some cut others torn from tissue paper, newsprint, envelopes, etc., are assembled on the support.

3 The papers are then arranged to divide the picture surface into broad areas of color and texture, simulating the light conditions of the harbor scene.

4 After the papers have been mounted with acrylic medium, the support is painted with clean water to soak the surface and prepare it for washes of colored inks.

5 Marine blue ink is applied to the damp surface with a broad bristle brush allowing rivulets of color to form.

6 While the blue ink is still wet, orange ink is applied, blended with the blue, and allowed to run.

7 The painting is allowed to dry before deciding what to do next.

8 White acrylic paint is rolled on in patches, creating areas of texture and allowing the colors beneath to show through.

9 A small palette knife is used to apply white accents to represent some of the house façades and the small boats lining the quay.

10 White highlights are scumbled on with a synthetic sable brush, adding more texture and simulating bright reflections on the water.

11 Orange ink is spattered onto the background by dragging the palette knife across the bristles of a toothbrush loaded with color.

12 A dipping pen is used with black ink to introduce line into the buildings and boat shapes. The artist uses both steel-nib and cut-bamboo pens.

13 Some spattered black ink has also been applied, reinforcing the lines and creating more texture.

14 To create more depth and richness, the artist has decided to apply additional washes of blue and orange to the background and harbor areas. This also introduces more tonal harmony. A 1-inch flat bristle brush is used.

15 Scraping away color with the tip of the palette knife. This exposes layers of color beneath and creates linear texture.

16 Thin cardboard dipped in acrylic white paint, and used edge on, is ideal for indicating the boat masts.

17 More patches of white texture are created by using the piece of cardboard flat.

18 Touches of pastel, usually the complementary color of the color beneath, are added to create "sparkle" and richness to the surface.

19 The finished painting.

GLOSSARY

Alla prima A technique of painting in which only one layer of paint is applied to a surface to complete a painting.

Binder The fixative with which powdered color is mixed.

Body color Pigments such as gouache that have been rendered opaque by the addition of a white substance like chalk.

Collage A work put together from assembled fragments.

Contre-jour Painting against the light.

Complementary colors Colors that lie opposite each other on the color wheel and have the effect of enhancing their opposite.

Fat Possessing a high proportion of oil to pigment.

Fugitive Applied to dyes and paints which are short-lived in intensity, especially in sunlight.

Glaze Transparent film of pigment over a lighter surface or over another.

Graffito Lines produced by scratching the pigmented surface to reveal another.

Gum arabic Hardened sap of acacia trees, used as a binder and to thicken paint and add gloss.

Hot pressed paper Paper produced by the "hot pressed" method.

Impasto Paint applied thickly, so that brush and palette knife marks are evident.

Lean Paint containing little oil in proportion to pigment.

Local color The inherent color hue of an object.

Luminosity The effect of light appearing to come from a surface.

Medium Substance mixed with pigment to make paint; and with acrylic and oil to ease manipulation.

Negative space The space around an object, which can be used as an entity in composition.

NOT Paper with a slightly textured surface, meaning "not" hot pressed.

Picture plane The defined surface area being painted.

Precipitation The grainy effect produced when pigment separates from the medium.

Pigment Coloring matter, the basis of paints, from natural or synthetic substances.

Resist Using materials which protect a surface from the action of paint; paper, masking tape, and masking fluid all fulfill this purpose.

Saturation The strongest possible concentration of pigment.

Scratching or scoring Lines etched into a paint surface with the tip of a palette knife or the handle of a paint brush.

Scumbling To drag or dab thick paint onto the support.

Spatial depth This is created by changing the tones of color on receding planes.

Sponging The application of paint with a natural sponge (preferably) to produce a textured surface.

Tint A color either diluted or mixed with white.

Tone The gradation of light to dark.

Tooth Texture or roughness of paper or canvas, allowing paint to grip the surface.

Unified colors Colors close together in the spectrum.

BIBLIOGRAPHY

Albert, Greg and Wolf, Rachel, *Basic Landscape Techniques* (in all mediums). North Light Books, 1993.

Harden, Elizabeth, *An Introduction to Painting Flowers*, Quintet Publishing Ltd, 1994.

Smith, Stan and Ted Holt, Professor H. F., *The Artist's Manual, Equipment, Materials, Techniques*, Macdonald Education Ltd, 1985.

Stephenson, Jonathan, *The Materials and Techniques of Painting*, Thames and Hudson, 1989.

INDEX

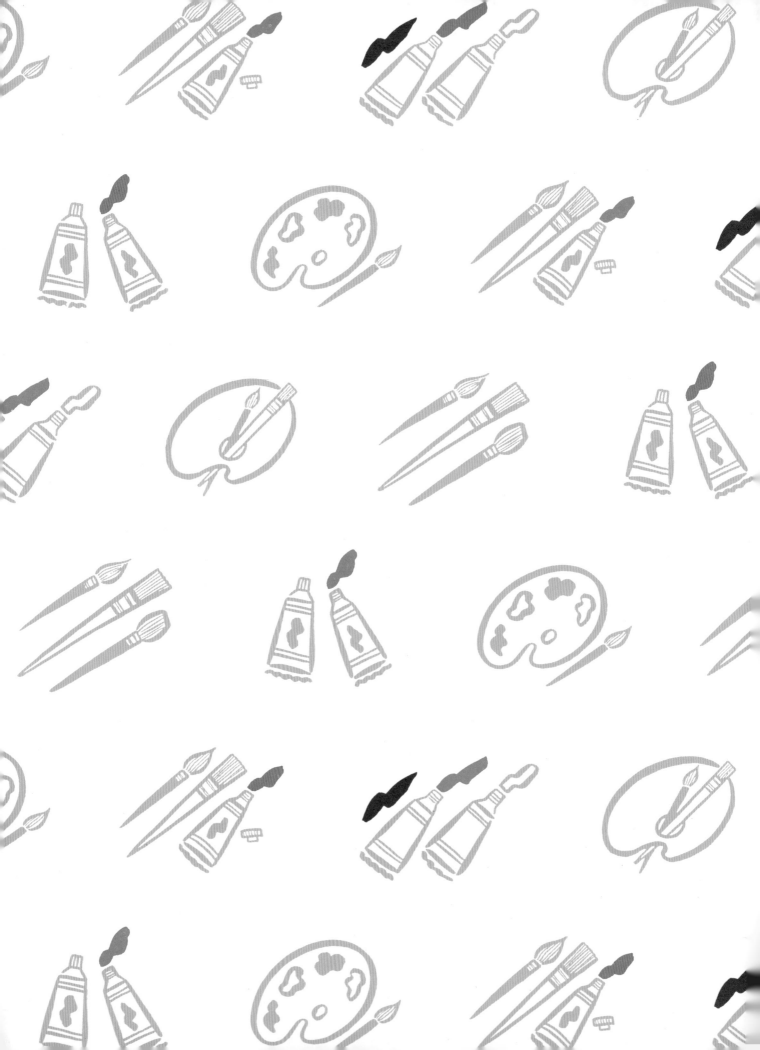